The imminent arrival of the new media technologies should change the priorities of contemporary philosophical inquiry and criticism. Whatever can be found lying around for potential deconstruction is from now on not so important as what is waiting to be constructed, for in Virtual Reality and other forms of new media, the map becomes the territory. Mark C. Taylor and Esa Saarinen's work is an antidote to an increasingly prevalent style of ~~...~~ that is inappropriately negative. It is much more courageous to construct new ide~~...~~ does so playfully, in order to confront the new media, and more importantly, to help create it. This is a book of imagination and craftsmanship; a work of responsible, and at this time necessary, generativity. How reactive and anemic other volleys in the cynicism race seem in comparison. **Jaron Lanier, Virtual Reality Pioneer**

**T**his book provides a necessary challenge to philosophy. Its reworking of both the presentation and form of philosophical thinking cannot be avoided. **Andrew Benjamin, University of Warwick**

**T**his profound and prescient

# "book"

enacts and enunciates a new philosophy of communication … a form and content of reflection that points to the role of philosophy in a global economy of telecommunications and micro-electronics. **Cornel West, Princeton University**

In this book, if I can call it that, Taylor and Saarinen have done much more than reflect on an experiment in creating a global classroom. They have raised profound questions about how we will talk to each other, work with each other, and live with each other in the visual electronic age that lies ahead. *Imagologies* gives us a peek into a brave new world whose social and political implications even Orwell never imagined. **Bill Weld, Governor of Massachusetts**

**I**t is almost a banality to say that the information age demands new paradigms for communications, in form as well as content. Yet the accuracy of the observation is driven home with a palpable energy and insight in this "book" by Mark Taylor and Esa Saarinen. Taylor and Saarinen conduct a verbal and visual dialogue, collage ideas, and develop insights within a framework and format that is simultaneously rigorous and spontaneous. This expansive text is not so much read as experienced. It is the work in the print medium that closely captures the process of creative development that generates from inspired associative thinking. **Thomas Krens, Director, The Guggenheim Museum**

As media and telecommunications networks expand with unprecedented speed, the very conditions of life are being transformed. No one has better grasped and as effectively conveyed the significance of these changes with more insight and vitality than Taylor and Saarinen. If you want to get a headstart on the 21st century, *Imagologies* is required reading.

**Terry Semel, President of Warner Brothers**

Here is an anti-book for the image age. By turns dazzling and affecting, technical and poignant, the virtually real authors sweep from economics to erotics, covering speed and space, money, the future of education, the role of the intellectual in the electronic age. We are all cyborgs now, plugged into our image machines … *Imagologies* synthesizes this new world order with savage candour, calling on us to wake up to the state of our own consciousness. It readies us for the next big stage of human evolution. The show is now on, and its hot. Don't miss it! **Colin McGinn, Rutgers University**

Time, space and emotional form are decisive factors in the energetic work of Mark Taylor and Esa Saarinen. This book of intelligence, sensitivity and courage is a visual and philosophical experience, rich in content, rich in graphic imagery. A beautiful work. **Jorma Uotinen, Director of the Finnish National Ballet**

A message from a new cultural era.

Post-Modernists are dead-on right about what's happening to us as we fall off the Millennial Cliff. Trouble is, they tend to express themselves in such a dense lingo that their valuable insights are unintelligible to any but themselves. I mean, cross a semiotician with a mobster and he'll make you an offer you can't understand. Mark Taylor and Esa Saarinen are different. By their conceptual rigor and originality, they have managed to retain the high respect of their obscure brethren and yet even a former cattle rancher like me knows what they are writing about. This makes them exceptionally rare and valuable. Read this book. It's not only possible, it's fun. **John Perry Barlow, Co-founder, Electronic Frontier Foundation**

Mark C. Taylor

Esa Saarinen

# iMAGOLOGIES

# MEDIA PHILOSOPHY

■

First published 1994

by Routledge

11 New Fetter Lane, London EC4P 4EE

■

Simultaneously published in the USA and Canada

by Routledge

29 West 35th Street, New York, NY 10001

■

Reprinted 1994, 1995, 1996

*Routledge is an International Thomson Publishing Company*

© 1994 Mark C. Taylor and Esa Saarinen

© Graphic design Marjaana Virta

Printed and bound in Great Britain by

Butler & Tanner Ltd, Frome and London

**British Library Cataloguing**

**in Publication Data**

A catalogue record for this book

is available from the British Library

**Library of Congress Cataloguing**

**in Publication Data**

A catalogue record for this book

is available from the Library of Congress

ISBN 0-415-10337-1 (hbk)

ISBN 0-415-10338-X (pbk)

■

**FOR**

Aaron, Kirsten
Oliver, Jerome

# IMAGOLOGIES

## Mark C. Taylor    Esa Saarinen

### MEDIA PHILOSOPHY

4

92952

IMAGO

Mark C. Taylor

M   E

PHILO

**Acknowledgments**

The educational experiment that provided the occasion for the reflections assembled in this "book" would not

have been possible without the cooperation of several institutions and businesses as well as many individuals.

We would like to express our sincere appreciation to the following: University of Helsinki and Williams College for

the willingness to support innovative pedagogical practices; Telecom Finland and Compression Labs,

**Mark C. Taylor**

Incorporated for providing the necessary equipment; Risto Huhta-Koivisto, Jouko Koivula, Mark Berman,

**Esa Saarinen**

Gemma Balukonis, and Bruce Wheat for technical assistance; our students: Jeff Allred, Joel Backström, Erin

**June 22, 1993**

Caddell, Ali Garbarini, Graham Gerst, Erkki Haapaniemi, Pekka Himanen, Harri Kantele, Matias Komulainen,

**To respond to this book, write:**

Cynthia Llamas, Brian Malone, Scott Miller, Kimmo Pentikäinen, Jon Stahl, Ari Tarjanne, Wayne Thomas, Dana

**Mark.C.Taylor@Williams.edu and**

Tomasino, Kaisu Virtanen and Jukka Ylitalo, for leading us into territory that is more theirs than ours; Rosa Liksom

**Esa.Saarinen@Helsinki.fi.**

for her irreverent presence; Margaret Bryant for everything; Antero Siljola, President of Werner Söderström

Corporation, and Williams College for technical and financial support necessary for the graphic design of the

book; the Academy of Finland and the Department of Philosophy, University of Helsinki for support of Saarinen's

research activities; and Francis Oakley, President, Williams College for his commitment to this project.

abcdefg
hijklm
mnopqr
stuvw
xyz åãó
'' ! ? £ —

# Communicative Practices

What our age needs is communicative intellect.   For intellect to be communicative, it must be active, practical, engaged.   In a culture of the simulacrum, the site of communicative engagement is electronic media.   In the mediatrix, praxis precedes theory, which always arrives too late.   The communicative intellect forgets the theory of communicative praxis in order to create a practice of communication.

Where would
Socrates hold his
dialogues today?
In the media and
on the net.

In simcult, the responsible writer must be an imagologist. Since image has displaced print as the primary medium for discourse, the public use of reason can no longer be limited to print culture. To be effective, writing must become imagoscription that is available to everyone.

The

electronetwork

that

mediaizes

the real

we

call

the

mediatrix.

# Transatlantic Cables:

September 4, 1991

# the first of the exchange

**Esa, it's Mark.**

Fine, fine. Yes, it has been too long, much too long. Things here are going very well. Too busy, of course, but it's always like that.

How is life in Helsinki? I trust the Queen and the boys are thriving.

So I've heard. News of some of your exploits has even made it to the States. It seems your involvement with the media is more intense than ever.

Listen, I have a suggestion for a totally different kind of media event. Let's team teach a course next fall.

I realize you can't get away from the university.

No, no, I don't have a leave and cannot come to Finland.  What I have in mind is something that has never before been done on an international scale.  Let's teach a seminar using the latest satellite or audio-visual telecommunications technology.  We would meet weekly with a group of students from Williams and Helsinki.  In addition to our class sessions, we would get everybody linked to the net.  This would enable us to have extended out-of-class contact and discussions.  **The Global Classroom** - that's the idea.  What do you think?

Yes, I agree, I think it is potentially a revolutionary undertaking.

Feasible?  I don't know; it must be.  Businesses and the media use this technology all the time.  Why can't we appropriate it for educational purposes?  Language shouldn't be a problem.  I am assuming your students could conduct discussions in English.  The Scandinavians' linguistic abilities put Americans to shame.

No, I haven't discussed it with anyone else.  I have no idea how much it would cost or how we would fund it.

Yeah, I figured it would be impossible to get support from the Finnish government or the University of Helsinki.  Finances are also pretty tight here at Williams.  But I don't think it is money we need.  It seems to me that this idea is interesting enough to attract corporate sponsorship.  If we can locate the right companies, I'll bet they would support this project.

Not yet.  But you have all kinds of contacts in the business community in Finland.  I have a friend who runs an outfit called Global Business Network.  Jay Ogilvy used to teach philosophy at Williams and is interested in the philosophical implications of electronic technology.  I'll ask him for some advice.  I'm sure he will be able to contact some educational consultants who can tell us whether this idea is totally off the wall.

We won't; I'll ask Jay to do it for nothing.

The subject of the seminar?  We'll have to work it out in detail but here's the general idea.  We could call the course "Imagologies" - something like mythologies but for images.  While writing my new book on twentieth-century art, architecture, and religion, I became fascinated by the growing role that images are playing in all aspects of contemporary life.  I am convinced that recent developments in electronic telecommunications technology have brought us to the brink of an extraordinary social and cultural revolution.  What is so remarkable is that the academy remains willfully blind to what is going on.  I suspect academics realize that the changes already under way call into question the very foundation upon which the university is built - print culture and everything that goes with it.  To make matters worse, the general public is largely unaware of what is at stake in recent technological developments.

I propose that we examine the broad-ranging implications of compu-telecommunications technology.  We could begin with some philosophical considerations of modern technology - you know, Heidegger, Baudrillard, Jameson, the usual stuff.  But then we could branch out into areas where this technology is having a major impact: media, writing, television and video, urban life, religion, economics, politics, war.  I don't know what else.  This approach would also give you the chance to reflect in a sustained way on your deep involvement in the Finnish media.  What would make this course unique would be the effort to bring together theory and practice by studying what we are doing and doing what we are studying.  This would enable us to engage in a radically new communicative practice while at the same time reflecting on our undertaking.  I believe the pedagogical significance of this project is enormous.  But the implications of such a venture reach far beyond the classroom - even if the classroom becomes global.  Our goal would be to create an awareness of the significance of the technological revolution that is taking place.  By conducting such a unique experiment, we would demonstrate what is already possible.  We must begin to think critically and creatively about this technology and start to shape our electronic environment in socially productive ways.

Super!  I knew this would be your kind of project.  Think it over, make a few inquiries, and let's talk again in a few days.

There is no communication without amplification. The question, then, is how best to achieve the amplification necessary for effective communicative practice. In simcult, print accomplishes less and less. Effective publication requires electronic amplification on a network that knows no bounds. The mediatrix allows high voltage communication-at-a-distance.

Expert language is a prison for knowledge and understanding. A prison for intellectually significant relationships. It is time to move beyond the institutional practices of triviledge, toward networks and surfaces, toward the play of superficiality, toward interstanding.

**Hi Mark, Esa here.**

Have to be quick, I'm in my car.  I have talked about the idea of a
teleseminar with some people and they are very enthusiastic.  Practical
problems seem enormous, however.  I am told that the Helsinki Telephone
Company has proper equipment as well as the Finnish Telecom.  Should be
quite sophisticated, their equipment.  How to persuade them to sponsor a
project like ours I don't know but maybe it can be done.  I know some
people from both companies and will pursue the matter further.  But how
will you get equipment for your end?

The diversity of language games appears as the diversity of media. Different media require different voices and different voices require different communicative strategies.

Brilliance is stupidity if it cannot communicate.

I've given public lectures in factories, banks, schools, to the Internal Revenue Service of Helsinki, for supermarket managers, lawyers, medical doctors, Mazda dealers, teachers, CEOs of big companies, social workers, the Bank of Finland, to personnel of mental hospitals. During the last few years, hundreds of such lectures. These lectures have reached perhaps tens of thousands of people, giving many of them their only relation to philosophy. This project takes seriously the naive assumption that philosophy matters.

Responsible thought cannot remain confined within the walls of the academy but must take to the street. In simcult, the street is the media. There is no reasonable alternative to electronic discourse.

Media and the net form a matrix of non-linear thinking and communication.

Good.  Same on this end.  I
finally got through to Ogilvy and
he thinks it is a great idea but
he is not optimistic about pulling
it off without a considerable
amount of money.  He said he knows
a couple of consultants who will
be able to give us good advice.
    I've also made some inquiries
about the kind of hardware we
would need.  It seems we have two
options.  We could use a satellite
connection.  I don't know if your
university has the necessary
equipment.  We are having a
satellite dish installed this
spring.  The problem is that we
will not have up-link capability.
I gather we could have a mobile
unit come to campus every week.
But that is very expensive -
something like $3,000.00 for each
session.  In addition to this, the
cost for satellite time ranges
from $8,600.00/hour (Panamsat) to
$18,600.00/hour (Intelsat).  If
our seminars run two hours each,
the cost for doing them by
satellite becomes prohibitive.
The other possibility is
audio-visual teleconferencing.
With this method, fiber optic
telephone lines are used to send
the signal.  The difficulty with
this option is that information
can only be transmitted in digital
form and therefore we would need a
machine that translates the
signals from analog to digital and
vice versa.  We would also have to
have dedicated phone lines between
Helsinki and Williamstown.  I have
no idea how much all of this would
cost.
    My initial impression is that
teleconferencing is the way to go.
The people at our Center for
Computing are very enthusiastic
about the project and have agreed
to provide whatever help they can.
They also think we ought to be
able to find a company to sponsor
it.  We are going to try to get
more information on the
teleconferencing alternative.  Can
you get in touch with people at
your computer or media center?
Perhaps they will have some other
ideas.
    Listen, do you have a fax
number?  Sometimes it's better to
send this stuff in writing.  Good.
I'll fax you the information when
I get it.
    OK.  As soon as possible.
Best to Pipsa.

It's Mark.
How are things going?

Practices[11]

September 22, 1991

**I**f your goal is to communicate, you must use whatever means you have at your disposal in a given situation. Communicative praxis must always be radically contextualized. In some circumstances, it is even necessary to use media against media to do what a given medium does not usually allow.

**I**nformation is not knowledge; knowledge is not understanding. How can we create understanding in a world in which information and knowledge are out of control?

**T**he challenge of imagologies is to transform institutional technologies dedicated to the production of information that is non-knowledge into institutional technologies dedicated to the production of knowledge that advances understanding. Understanding presupposes information and knowledge but information and knowledge less and less lead to understanding. Communicative practice transforms the information and knowledge of simcult into a new understanding that is transformative.

in a culture of the simulacrum, communicative practice is necessarily theatrical. Electronic media are instrumental in staging an exchange in which the currency of information makes understanding possible.

The only responsible intellectual is one who is wired.

imagology involves a second naiveté in which the figural, which has too long been repressed by the conceptual, returns as the medium for understanding and communication. The return of figure disfigures the disfiguration of concepts by reinscribing the imago in the midst of the logos.

paradox of the imaginary register: the proliferation of images is iconoclastic.

Simcult

**P**ostmodern
society is radically decentered
and thoroughly disseminated. As a
result of this dispersion, the machine of
socio - cultural reproduction is no longer
controlled by centralized agencies. Center and
hierarchy give way to periphery and horizontality,
creating a lateral expanse that extends endlessly in
undefined directions. In the absence of centralized
and hierarchical control, localized interventions in
the structures of cultural reproduction and
social production become not only
entertainable but sometimes
even entertaining.

In simcult, excess becomes excessive.

**Mark?  Esa.**

I've talked
with people at
the university
who have used
videoconferencing
techniques for
transmitting
lectures.  We
have equipment
but it won't be
sufficient for
us.  We need
two-way capacity.
My feeling is
that the Finnish
Telecom would be
an excellent
partner in this
effort.  They
are breaking
some innovative
ground in project
development and
I've done some
lectures and
consulting for
them.  But I
don't want to
push on too
strongly before
we have the
thing more
concretely
figured out.
Please continue
moving forward
at your end.

To appreciate Baudrillard's analysis of the culture of the simulacrum, it is necessary to understand the sources of his thought. The most obvious influence on Baudrillard is Guy Debord's **The Society of Spectacle.** A situationist, Debord recognized both the strengths and the weaknesses of Marx's position.  While Marx developed a sophisticated interpretation of the relation between socio-cultural processes and economic dynamics, his analysis is not directly applicable to post-industrial capitalism. With the advent of consumer society, culture itself becomes commodified.  The commodification of the sign makes it necessary to develop a semiology that is missing in Marx. This is one of the tasks that Debord sets for himself in his seminal work. A less obvious precursor of Baudrillard's account of the society of spectacle is Marx's archrival, Hegel. When Marx inverted Hegelian idealism to form a materialistic account of the infrastructure of ideological constructs, he turned away from some of the most important insights developed in speculative philosophy. Appearances to the contrary notwithstanding, the society of spectacle is the concrete realization of speculative philosophy.   While Hegel's whole philosophical enterprise is dedicated to translating images into concepts, the society of spectacle is immersed in images in such a way that concepts always appear to be figurative.   Nonetheless, Hegel's speculative idealism anticipates the society of spectacle's idealism of the image. According to Hegel, the concept is actually embodied in space and time.  In different terms, objectivity is actually conceptual or the real is the idea.  In the society of spectacle, the idea becomes the image and the real is imaginary.  For Hegel, it is concept all the way down; for the society of spectacle, it is image all the way down.   In the twentieth century, the Hegelian concept becomes real in electronic telecommunications.   The net wires the world for Hegelian **Geist**.

**P**ower becomes imaginary.

**D**isillusion is impossible when the real is imaginary. Illusion gives way to illusion to create a hall of mirrors in which there is no exit. To survive in simcult, one must learn to live the impossibility of dis-illusionment.

**I**n the culture of the simulacrum, everything becomes current and only currency is "real."

**T**he threat of simcult is that outrage becomes unfashionable.

**S**imcult presupposes the commodification of commodification.

## October 1, 1991

## Dear Esa,

I must confess that I am feeling a bit down at the moment. Ogilvy got back to me with the report from his consultants. They say that we are five years ahead of the times unless we have about $200,000. My response was that it is precisely because we are five years ahead of the times that we must do it now. What makes this project so interesting is that it has never before been done. I believe we have an opportunity to pioneer a new form of international education.

Armed with Ogilvy's report, I went to the director of our development office. I explained the project and indicated your interest as well as the enthusiasm of the people at our Center for Computing. His first question, of course, was: "How much will it cost?" I told him what Ogilvy had said but stressed that I thought we could find companies to sponsor the experiment. What we need, I explained, is not money but help in finding potential sponsors. To say that he was not receptive to the idea would be an understatement. Stressing that the college is in the midst of a major capital campaign, he said he simply did not have the time for such a limited undertaking. While admitting that the proposal is interesting, he said he was not sure the timing was right. What I find remarkable about this response is the lack of vision.

In the face of all of these obstacles, I am not sure what to do. What do you think?

# In simcult, the essential is nothing

**S**imcult is a culture of instrumentality and nothing but instrumentality. Precisely the lack of any end-in-itself makes it all the more urgent to fabricate ends carefully. Instead of proclaiming the end of technology, we need to refashion the management of ends. End-production is not a terminal condition but is a creative beginning.

**T**he play of the simulacrum creates a lite culture.

**Dear Mark,**

    Got  your  fax,  doesn't  seem  too  good.  Pisses  me  off,  those
key  thing  is  to  maintain  the  spark  of  craziness.  We'll  figure

# and nothing is essential.

**S**imcult engenders an air of information.

**i**n the inverted economy of simcult, the **imago dei** becomes the **deus imaginis.**

```
academics.  But let's proceed.  With a project like this, the
out something.
```

**P**ostmodernism marks the end of liberalism.
1. The individual is no longer the primary locus of meaning or agent of action.
2. The opposition between the public and the private collapses.
And yet, you must still face others.

When every foundation is imaginary, alienation becomes impossible.

But this does not mean that reconciliation is possible.

**S**imcult     is     fandom.

Modernism idealizes the universality and homogeneity required by industrial capitalism. Modern capitalism involves processes of centralization that presuppose mass production and mass consumption. The media played a central role in the creation and maintenance of the culture of homogeneity. From newspapers and magazines to radio and television, economic processes were regulated by creating a universal code for uniform interests.

Postmodernism idealizes the singularity and heterogeneity required by post-industrial capitalism. Postmodern capitalism involves processes of decentralization that presuppose diverse modes of production and pluralized forms of consumption. The media play a central role in the creation and maintenance of the culture of heterogeneity. From hypertexts and email to video and virtual reality, economic processes are regulated by creating multiple codes for local interests.

Postmodernism does not, however, simply negate modernism. To the contrary, the universality and homogeneity of modernism constitute the mediatrix that creates the possibility of articulating the singularity and heterogeneity of postmodernism. Universality engenders singularity even as heterogeneity presupposes homogeneity.

The register of the imaginary is

Images proliferate, the net spreads, the volume rises. No one is in control.

In simcult, elision is not illusion.

Does postmodernism inevitably destroy the pathos of modernism? Can the dreams of modernism be refigured in a culture of the simulacrum? Can the energy of modernism be regenerated in the midst of postmodern irony and cynicism? Can art become life and life become art in more revolutionary and productive ways than modernism ever dreamed?

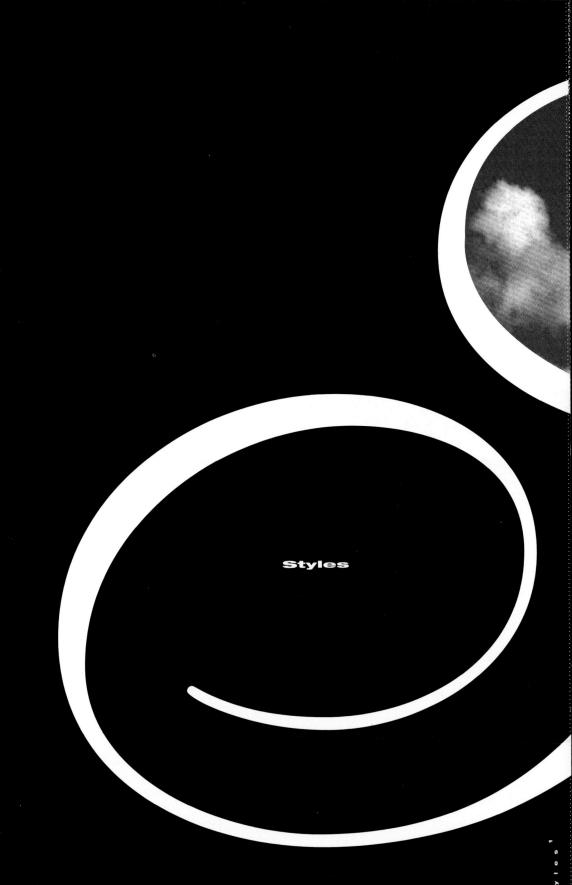

# Styles

**Esa - -**

OK.

Let's go for it.  If we pull it off, they

will be the first to try to cash in on it.

It's too interesting a possibility to give

up because others do not appreciate what

is at stake.

**October 6, 1991**

in simcult, substance **is** style and style **is** substance.

The challenge is not to make statements but to ask questions. The imagologist does not trade securities but trafficks in insecurities. When the currency of the realm is insecure, the economies of reflection are constantly shifting.

imagology insists that the word is never simply a word but is always also an image. The audio-visual trace of the word involves an inescapable materiality that can be thought only if it is figured. The abiding question for conceptual reflection is:

**How to (dis)figure the wor(l)d?**

The fragmentary is no longer simply a literary style. The literary fragment was the invention of the Romantics for whom it presupposed an entire metaphysics. One of the paradoxes of modern literary and philosophical history is that the metaphysics of the fragment is not itself fragmentary. The trope that embodies the metaphysics of the fragment is the synecdoche.

For postmoderns the fragmentary has become a psycho-socio-cultural condition. It is no longer a question of whether or not to write fragments, for the fragmentary has become our destiny. Even texts that attempt to avoid or repress the fragmentary end by fragmenting themselves. It is, of course, possible to attempt deliberately to compose fragments. But what is the difference between a fragment that is intended to be a fragment and a fragment that is a fragment

# malgré lui?

Perhaps the unintended fragment is more fragmented than the intended fragment.

Whether intended or unintended, the postmodern fragment calls into question the metaphysics of the modern fragment. And yet, can postmodern fragmentary styles elude the structures of metaphysics? To elude is not to escape. Even though there is no exit from metaphysics, the metaphysical is not necessarily all-encompassing, totalizing, or exhaustive. To write fragments that are not modern would be to remain forever elusive.

**W**hat
does
it
mean
to
write
with
sound
or
even
with
smell?

**W**hile marking the closure of the western metaphysical tradition, deconstruction also signals the opening of post-print culture. Deconstruction remains bound to and by the world of print that it nonetheless calls into question. What comes after deconstruction? Imagology. To realize what deconstruction has made possible, it is necessary to move into the world of telecommunications technology. The notion of textuality cannot be radicalized until it is transformed from print to other media. To perform dissemination is to electrify the signifier.

**Esa, it's Mark.**

I'm going to be in France for a few days next
week.  Is there any chance you could come down to
Paris for an afternoon to discuss the seminar?  I
think we are at a point where such a meeting would
be helpful.  There are many details that we need to
work out if we are going to get this thing off the
ground.

**H**ypertexts free the **play** of signs that has always constituted writing. This play is both trivial and deadly serious.

Lighten up so you can get serious.
Get serious so you can lighten up.

**N**ot complete, not direct, not thorough, but brief, quick and allusive – like a fleeting blip on a video screen.

**S**tyles are not only written; they must also be lived. To embody style is to incarnate the **imago** in all dimensions of one's life. Image is destiny, which sometimes can be changed.

**E**sa's polka-dot shoes are a Warhol painting that has come to life. Style – all the way down to his very sole.

**October 26, 1991**

## Hi Mark, Esa.

OK, I've checked my schedule and the planes and it seems I can take the morning flight in on Friday, November 1st. I'll see you at noon. Let's say at Café Select on Boulevard Montparnasse. That's opposite La Coupole. We'll have about three hours because I've arranged to meet some other people as well before I take the evening flight back. See you in Paris on Friday.

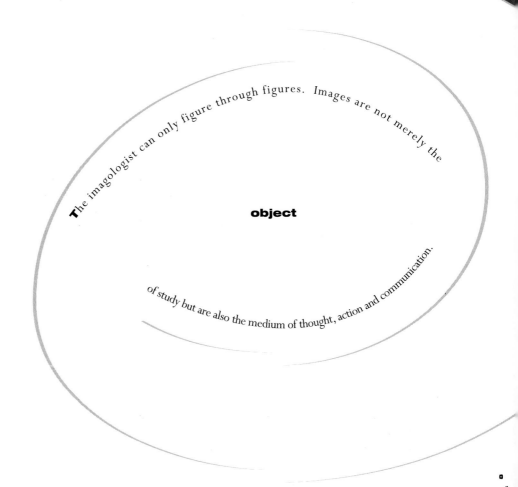

The imagologist can only figure through figures. Images are not merely the

**object**

of study but are also the medium of thought, action and communication.

imagologies follow the lead of deconstruction by giving up the search for secure foundations. The disappearance of the signified in the endless field of signifiers is embraced as an unavoidable cultural condition. This destiny should not be suffered with a heavy heart but affirmed in all its creative richness.

The imagologist suffers from the mania for signifying.

Style has never been mere ornament. The text believed to be straightforward and ornament-free simply displays the machine aesthetic of functional simplicity. In telewriting, the inevitability of style becomes self-conscious. To write is to stylize even when we deny it. In this way, telewriting rediscovers the style hidden in every stylus.

The book of media philosophy is a scrapbook made up of "philosophical fragments" that constitute an unconcluding unscientific postscript to every system of interpretation. In the post-age, all writing is a post-script.

N A I V E

**N**aiveté requires a Kierkegaardian leap of faith in the age of faithlessness. Through this leap, we land precisely where we were already standing and yet are thoroughly transformed.

The play of surfaces exposes
depth as another surface. In the
absence of depth, the
hermeneutics of suspicion
becomes impossible and second
naiveté unavoidable.

Scientific truth always comes too late.

# N

**Dear Esa,**

Very, very good news. Compression Labs Incorporated in San Diego will loan us the teleconferencing equipment free of charge. The machine we need is called a Codex (coder-decoder). The model CLI will loan us is the Rembrandt 2-06. We must pay to have the equipment connected and disconnected. In addition to this, we must cover the cost of the telephone lines. But use of the equipment without charge represents a major step forward. I am sending a copy of the letter of agreement.

Several questions must be addressed. First, can you get money to cover the installation, deinstallation and shipping on the Helsinki end? Second, and more important, do you think that the Helsinki phone company could be persuaded to donate use of the necessary communication lines? I seem to recall you mentioning that you have some connections at the phone company. The kind of line we need is: 112 kilobytes/second digital telephone link. I have no idea what this means or involves. We are investigating the possibility of an American company donating use of the lines. We are also trying to find out how much it would cost if we have to rent the lines. If we must pay for the lines, could you find the money from the university or from private sources to cover half of the cost?

I also need to know the exact dates of your fall semester. The company will have to know when we will use the equipment.

I was beginning to get discouraged but this is a real breakthrough. Give me a call to let me know what you think about all of this.

Naiveté 2

**M**edia philosophy is philosophy for children. But what does it mean to be **for children**? To philosophize **for children** is to philosophize in such a way that kids tune to your channel. You must, therefore, dare to be naive and superficial by talking their language and not trying to impose your concepts on them. But to be for children is also to be willing to accept responsibility for creating and sustaining structures and networks to support life. In simcult, this means that we must act to shape and reshape the telecommunications environment that is the world in which our children are destined to dwell.

**December 20, 1991**

**Hi Mark, Esa here.**

    Dynamite news.  I've met with the CEO of the Finnish Telecom and he has
agreed, in principle, to sponsor the project.  He is going to ask his
technical people to check the costs, before a definite answer, but I am
very optimistic.  Anyway, because of the time difference we could use
their studio after office hours free of charge.  How we'll get Telecom's
technical people to look after the show after hours I don't know but
maybe that can be solved.  I'm going to meet with them for a demo early
in January.

In a culture of potential ecocatastrophe, academic neutrality paves the way for a polite, silent rape. What is needed is the strength of vision for the obvious.

One of the most perplexing problems we face is how to think historically in an age that has forgotten history. If history is over, to raise the question of the historical seems embarrassingly naive. Nonetheless, at least one question still seems legitimate: What **are** the historical conditions of the end of history?

Except you become as little children, you cannot ↑ enter the kingdom of the simulacrum.

For Europeans, the fascination with America arises from Americans' complete lack of sophistication. For Americans, Europe is Grandma's house and doesn't know it.

(Brian)

laughable project: not to analyze but to explode language in an effort to create tentative syntheses of that-which-cannot-be-synthesized.

# MEDiA

**Philosophy**

Philosophy has been constructed to repress precisely what media philosophy solicits —

image, artifice and simulacrum. The transformation enacted in media philosophy is not a

simple reversal that imitates through opposition. To the contrary, media philosophy opens

a new space for philosophical reflection that previously has been unavailable. At this

moment, it is not possible to define this space with any precision; nor will it be possible

to describe it before entering it. The experiment in which we are engaged is a venture

into this new space that awaits us. Only after crossing the threshold of cyberspace might

we begin to discern the unthought possibilities of philosophy in our day.

For philosophy, imagology is the return of the repressed.

Public

use of

reason

in the

age of

media is

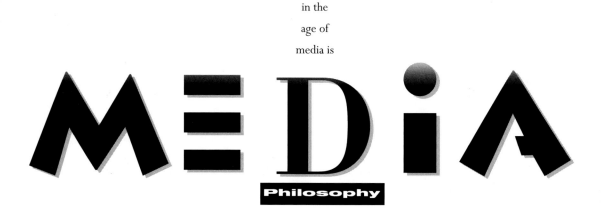

Philosophy

**P**erhaps the roots of our project can be traced farther back than either of us has realized. Kierkegaard, after all, was the first philosopher to realize the importance of the media. He insisted that the mass media of his day – primarily the press – transformed responsible individuals into passive ciphers. By developing an edifying philosophy, Kierkegaard attempted to call people back to themselves by providing the occasion for the self-consciousness necessary for autonomous individuality.

There is, however, another aspect of Kierkegaard's work that anticipates media philosophy. In his aesthetic authorship, he creates contrasting personae who project imaginary worlds. Each of the pseudonymous texts embodies a different form of life. The style of the writing reflects the style of life and vice versa. When composing his aesthetic works, Kierkegaard did not remain cloistered in his study but took to the streets in an effort to create a public image that would advance his religio-philosophical enterprise. He described his complex strategy as indirect communication.▶▶▶▶▶

▶ If the street has now become the mediatrix, then to remain faithful to Kierkegaard, it would be necessary for philosophy to take to the airwaves, cables and satellites. Scandinavia and America meet somewhere over or under the Atlantic. When understood in this way, media philosophy extends Kierkegaard's aesthetic authorship into the electronic age.

is  media  philosophy.

The  text  publicizes  the  global  classroom,  which,  in  turn,  publicizes  the  text.

images      must      be      inhabited      not      simply      interpreted.

I went to Boston yesterday for the demonstration. It really does help to see the technology in action. This will be something else if we can pull it off.

In general, I was encouraged by my discussions. On the question of phone lines, there should be no problem. It is my understanding that Finnish Telecommunications will cover costs of sending the signal from Helsinki. I have a dedicated line to Springfield, MA, which is where the international lines come in.

There are three options for data transmission: 56, 112 and 384 kilobytes/second. As the number goes up, so do the price and resolution. Since there will not be much motion in the seminar, I think we can get away with 112 kbs/second. This will make the cost more manageable. There will be some visual distortion but it won't be too bad.

The only question concerns the compatibility of the telecommunications equipment. As you know, CLI has agreed to loan us the Codex for the cost of installation and deinstallation. If we use this, there won't be any problems for us. But you indicated that you had free access to other equipment. AT&T people said that they thought it would be Picture-Tel, which is not compatible with CLI. It is possible to make it compatible but each of us would need a $10,000 piece of equipment. Furthermore, transmission costs are greater. If I were to get Picture-Tel equipment, it would cost $4,200.000 for each 30 days. There is also a $4,000 installation/deinstallation fee. It would be difficult to come up with this money. I don't know if we have a problem here or not. When you have your demonstration, ask them the following questions:

1. Is the system dial-up or reservation? Dial-up is much better for us.

2. Which vendor, system, revision and software are you using?

3. Get the name and phone number of a person at your phone company who can talk with my AT&T representative. We have to get some of these people talking directly so we don't screw everything up in translating it.

Let's talk Thursday or Friday.

I am going to send you several books I think we could use. We must decide on texts because my book orders for the fall term must be placed in June.

Making headway - hang tough!

**W**hy imagologies? Why media philosophy? Because even in a postmodern age, we must continue to speak and act in an effort to make a difference. An adequate philosophy for the postmodern age will refuse to endure the status quo – the cool postmodern cynicism with its history-has-ended and agony-in-indifference.

Media philosophy is an attack on the institutions of rational, systematic, uncommercial, analytic, supposedly value-free, unmediated, objective thought. It sets itself against every form of critical thought that remains a prisoner to the abstract.

In the media, one-liners are everything. Impressions are everything. Style, personality and a timing are everything. There is no possibility – and this cannot be emphasized too much – of ruling out the scholar's nightmare of ambiguity and, even more shocking, radical, outraged, emotionally charged misunderstanding. For those who still believe in the dream of transparent intersubjectivity or an ideal speech community of the experts who trade clear and distinct ideas, essences and concepts, misunderstanding constitutes an abiding fear. But misunderstanding can release energy. The law of the media is the law of dirty hands: you cannot be understood if you are not misunderstood.

In the media, the autonomous cogito is torn to pieces. Attacked, disregarded, loved and envied, the subject finally has to live at the mercy of others. What is distasteful for the philosopher is not the encounter with the other but the character of the others encountered. Those one meets in the media are not the abstract others of elegant, highbrow philosophy but the farting others of the supermarkets and public toilets – the unheroic and intellectually distasteful taxpaying masses. To be at the mercy of customers, consumers – that's the horrid part of media philosophy. To be subjected to unavoidable misunderstandings, formed by the ridiculous, laughable, unlettered and unsophisticated rednecks, most of whom have never read one single page of any **"**groundbreaking volume**"** of this century or any other century – that's the condition of media philosophy. In this context, our most developed and esteemed cognitive machinery suddenly seems hopelessly outdated. The more sophisticated the tactical arsenal, the less useful it becomes. The more it draws from history, from classics, the less force and creative energy it has. In simcult, Marx's famous thesis on Feuerbach must be revised: Philosophers have interpreted the world; the point is to change the images through which we live.

The mediatrix cannot be trusted. It's always fooling around. And yet, it is the milieu that nourishes us.

**P**hilosophy has rejected its initial promise to forward a critical, creative, space in an effort to become an ordered and disciplined, stylized surface of linear,

**M**edia philosophy transforms the philosophy of language into an energetics of image. A word is a micropower that carries political force. It is a mistake to believe that a word introduces itself primarily as a concept-with-a-metaphysics. Metaphysics is secondary to politics, praxis, erotics and powerplay. This shift in understanding linguistic force is highlighted in imagologies where metaphysics is absent. Or, perhaps more accurately, where the metaphysics is flat. The immanence of energy remains and networks of simulacra proceed as structures of power. Consequently, the media philosopher does not take words, concepts, ideational analysis and even philosophy itself all that seriously. Language does not set the limits of the world because the world does not have any fixed limits but is an ongoing project of the imagination.

**Dear Mark,**

The demo at the Finnish Telecom
went beautifully.  Great guys to
work with.  They have three types of
transmission intensities - if that
is the term - but I think we will
survive with the cheapest, which,
incredibly, takes only two telephone
lines.  Thus, the cost of running
the show will be cut to a minimum if
we can just get the two studios to
talk to one another.  That's the
main worry now - Finnish Telecom
doesn't use CLI equipment.  The big
news, however, is that the Finnish
Telecom guys will donate the use of
the phone lines.  I may have to do
some lectures for them but that's
OK, I like these guys.

# **P e t r a**

# Kelly

and Gerd Bastian, her longtime companion, were found shot dead in their home in Bonn; their bodies were partly decomposed. No signs of violence, the police say. Apparently Bastian, an ex-army officer who became disillusioned with the military and turned into a spokesman for the German Green movement, first shot Kelly in the head and then killed himself. A joint suicide? No political testament or declaration was found.

I met the Green superstars in 1987. The Finnish Green movement had organized a big happening at the National Theater on the same night as the government was running a televised seminar on "Structural Change in Control," which involved many institutionally powerful people. The National Theater was packed; the atmosphere was tense and challenging. I gave a speech entitled "Give Me Fatherland," which was greeted by a volcano of excited applause. The main speaker was Kelly, who was the symbol for the international Green movement. She was feeling dead tired, after having worked under great pressure for many months. Nevertheless, her speech, delivered without notes, was brilliant, eloquent, forceful, touching. She displayed tremendous charisma and an extraordinary aura of deeply felt convictions. Kelly created a magical field of courage and hope that effectively personalized the Green movement. As a media figure, she was a powerful and ingenious marketer of Green ideology. She brought the German Green party stunning breakthrough victories in the 1980s and, by so doing, set in motion major developments elsewhere in Europe. Yet soon after her most spectacular successes, the Green party refused to support her candidacy for parliament. The party decided that "the personality cult" had to be fought at any cost. What was the cost? Today the German Green party does not hold a single seat in the German parliament.

The tragedy of Petra Kelly is the tragedy of morality in the media age. The old-fashioned intelligentsia cannot take command of media technologies. Unable to make use of the instruments of postmodern warfare, Pure Reason, Pure Morality and Pure Politics remain captive to the technologies they abstractly oppose. The old order represses criticism and remains idiotically self-satisfied in its apparently forceful effort "to stay away from the dirt of the media." Petra Kelly was destroyed by her own people. Media philosophy must prepare itself for a similar drama.

In the mediatrix, you throw yourself to others. You create through others. The media philosopher realizes painfully that she must sacrifice her beloved cogito, her cherished institutionalism, her age-old desire for total control to a communal process-in-the-making.

**M**edia provide the ultimate shock for the prisoners of institutionalized philosophy. So great is the fear of the public that even print media must be immunized against infection from outsiders before philosophers will contemplate their use. Fearing the gaze of the public, academic philosophy trivializes with a "sophistication" that destroys any communal and moral stand before the agonies of the so-called outside world.

**P**referring a life in the shadows, most philosophers do not want to encounter the gaze of others. They avoid the challenge of the most demanding artwork: oneself. Foucault is right when he notes that the western tradition is unusual in its limitation of artworks to external physical products that are exhibited in museums. Media philosophy insists that one must take his or her life seriously as being-for-the-other in the space of spectacle. You speak to others and to yourself through the media. Philosophy in the media is revolutionary for the standard practice of philosophy precisely because it insists on the importance of a surface energy that the tradition has done everything it can to abolish. From the point of view of school philosophy, "surface" and "energy" are notions of no consequence because the serious, intellectually institutionalized philosopher is a servant of depth and eternity, content and pure logic. In media, by contrast, surface energy is everything.

**M**edia philosophy rejects analytics in favor of communication. Explosive, outrageous communication is the lifeblood of hope in the world of simulacra, bureaucracy and collapsing ecosystems.

The imagologist must not fear banality but exploit it.

When a traditional philosopher observes the performance of a media philosopher he sighs: "Fashion, mere fashion. It will pass. Better to avoid the fleeting and devote oneself to the abiding." But while he waits, what passes is the fashion of the abiding.

The media — as opposed to money or other assets — have become the Ultimate Capital. Ultimate capital is also the ultimate fetish, which becomes the ultimate object of envy. Critics denounce the media as "capitalistic manipulation machinery" and "mechanisms of nihiliation." But the ultimate capital is also the ultimate power. We must learn how to tap this power. The fate of philosophy in the twenty-first century will be judged by its ability to turn into media philosophy.

Deconstruction is an ingenious continuation of the critical function of philosophy. It does not render obsolete philosophy's synthetic function, which any serious student of the contemporary must address with full force. In the age of the fragmentary, with its exponentially increasing administrative and technical structures, the synthetic function of philosophy must loom large. This is not a call for totalizing discourse of the kind criticized by leading theorists of the postmodern, but is an appeal to undertake the effort to discern connections and interrelations for the purpose of evaluation and intervention.

The articulative function of philosophy no longer can live in the academic chambers of institutionalized discourse. Articulation in the media means articulation outside the shelter of institutionalized reason. At the same time that discursive practices of articulation undergo a profound change, the politics and moralities that constitute the basis of motivation are transformed. In simcult, articulation serves a function different from what it has served in expert-cultures of the past. The colonization of the critical, synthetic and articulative by scholarly and abstracto-expertized ways of constituting a "serious" subject matter is what media philosophy sets out to fight. To pursue this course means opening the door to radically local, transient and idiosyncratic philosophical strategies. Media philosophy defines methods of communally touching, frightening and enlightening with critical, synthetic and articulative force. Methods will vary from time to time and place to place. The tactics of a Finn in Finland today will not necessarily serve a would-be media-philosophic superstar in LA or Stuttgart twenty years from now.

The erotics of media philosophy are predominantly female, having to do with sensualities, impressions, continuities, subtleties and dispersed orgasms. Such polymorphous perversity is, nonetheless, made possible by an infrastructure of aggressive and goal-directed male erotics with ultra-speedy transmissions and sudden climaxes.

Once the mediatrix touches you, subjectivity explodes into a high-energy awareness of its own objectivity. You become an image in front of millions and in front of yourself. The otherness of the image both frightens and inspires.

**M**edia    philosophy    must    be    mobile,    manipulative,    manic.

**I**n simcult, the political and cultural responsibility of philosophy is measured in the media rather than in the world of academia. As the foundations of linear thinking, cumulative history and pure thought collapse under the reign of media, little is left of what we teach or learn in PhD programs. The challenge is to create a vision that sells, a criticism that magnetizes, a product-line that delivers technologically advanced products for an age that will not survive without explosive new thinking, analysis and synthesis.

**April 4, 1992**

**Esa –**

    Great news!  But
my technical
people tell me the
compatibility
problem still is
not solved.  In
the States, we
operate in
56-kilobyte
chunks.
Therefore, we need
two phone lines to
get the 112
kilobytes we need.
In Europe, you use
64-kilobyte
chunks.  To make
our systems
compatible, you
have to get a data
module that will
reduce
transmission from
64 to 56 kilobytes
per second.  Do
you think you can
work this out?

**A** colleague from another department complained:
"All those students queue for your lectures simply
because you're in the gossip columns and they want
to hear if you again speak of Pipsa." "That's an
excellent reason to come to a philosophy lecture," I
said.

**I**n media philosophy, performance displaces truth.

**M**adonna is one of the foremost imagologists in the world today. She ingeniously imposes new meaning on female subjectivity by the self-controlled use of mythical and imaginal strategies. Her collage techniques are a beautiful example of postmodern possibilities. Madonna is **posing-for**. Posing-for lies at the heart of postmodern energies in a world where original subject categories like "authority," "sovereignty" and "consciousness as cogito" have lost their creative potential.

Postmodernity is **posing-for**. Even the dignified gravity of history is ripped off by techniques of indifference, collage and quotation. In the postmodern, if history is to have any momentum, it must humiliate itself into a posing-for. This posing-for, so superbly managed by Madonna, hits with lethal force at the heart of print culture. In the culture of print, reason has invested its feeble energies in the lukewarm and ridiculous list of the alphabet. Once institutionalized, the alphabet denies its status as posing-for. But you cannot reach tomorrow without freely embracing the culture of posing-for. The very strategies, techniques, institutions, conceptions and situational praxes of reason must be reevaluated in the face of posing-for. Posing-for is a quantum leap into the visual, the image, the simulacrum. Madonnaized philosophy involves quoting and citing, without respect for content but with ultimate care for posing-for, pornographicized objectivism taken as techniques of subjectification. Speed, flash, exaggeration. Excesses, excesses, excesses – not in theories, abstractions and conceptualizations but in posing-for.

**M**edia philosophy is thoroughly theatrical. The challenge is to stage the signifier endlessly.

in our era, we must philosophize with images rather than concepts.

Municipal elections here in Finland. I sleep late, waking up at 11:00 with Pipsa and the boys. We talk and giggle in bed for a while until the phone rings. It's a journalist from the national TV, wanting to interview me for their broadcast on the results of the election. I haven't checked the outcome yet and won't check until the last minute. In the media, it is essential to keep fresh. Reading the newspapers in the taxi on the way to the studio, I carry forward the project of dynamic superficialities.

in media philosophy,

# impressions

count more than intelligence.

**Dear Esa,**

The technical problems we have been having are fascinating and important. So often in recent weeks we have seemed very close to completing the circuit and making the connection. But each time there is one more adaptation necessary to make your plug fit our socket and our plug fit your socket. It seems obvious that the logic of this technology points toward standardization and homogenization. And yet, the companies producing the technology resist the very logic their machines require because they are afraid of losing their competitive advantage.

In the long run, the logic of standardization will carry the day. There are, of course, serious problems with such standardization, ranging from the technological to the political. On the technological level, standardization creates vulnerability. Consider, for example, an analogy drawn from the domain of physical organisms. One of the most effective defenses against disease and infection is biodiversity. Differences among organisms make certain species vulnerable to some diseases but resistant to others. If all organisms had the same genetic constitution, it would be possible for a single virus to wipe out an entire species. The standardization of electronic technology poses a similar threat. It is no accident that the term "virus" has been transferred from biology to computers. Computer viruses work the same way as biological viruses. A biological virus, which is a portion of genetic code, invades an organism and turns its replicating processes against the host to reproduce an infecting parasite. In a similar manner, a computer virus invades the electronic system and appropriates the computer's replicating processes to destroy its host. In the absence of techno-diversity, it becomes difficult, if not impossible, to stop the spread of disease.

It does not take much imagination to envision the catastrophic consequences of such a prospect. For example, what if a virus invades the electronic network that constitutes the global economy? The standardization of technology creates the possibility of a market crash of unprecedented proportions. Moreover, there might be no recovery from such a crash, for "money" itself would disappear with the programs.

The disturbing political ramifications of the logic of standardization have already become painfully obvious in the course of this century. Standardization and homogenization can lead to totalitarianism. If the real is defined as that which is the same, then difference appears to be something like a virus that must be exterminated. The ways in which societies attempt to inoculate themselves against infection from the outside vary from time to time and place to place. Electronic telecommunication raises the prospect of surveillance and repression on an unprecedented scale. There are, however, certain checks and balances that accompany technological standardization. Most important, the very process of standardization also decentralizes the communication network. With decentralization, the concentration of power in the machines of a few becomes more and more difficult. Hackers expose the weakness of the techno-web that seems so overpowering. It would be a mistake to fail to appreciate the political significance of hackers. Their subversive activity not only exposes the holes in the net but also underscores the importance of resistance to the homogenization that nonetheless cannot be stopped.

It has become clear that our project cannot proceed without standardization. And yet, the very standardization necessary for global communication might eventually be what leads to the breakdown of the circuits linking us all.

**May 1, 1992**

**A**merica is at its most exciting when it does not theorize, articulate, or conceptualize, but when it acts. America's philosophy is pragmatism, but not in its theoretical, conceptualized form. As we reflect on the borders and possibilities of philosophy in the electronic era, three points emerge:

**1** In the praxis-dominated world of ultra-tech, the politics of critique must take a new form. ●

**2** The strength of theory is relative to strategies for action. Action must lead, theory must follow. In opposition to mainstream modern western philosophy, theoretical and conceptual reason must serve only an instrumental role and thus give up its previously unchallenged position of supreme value in itself. ●

**3** Critique that is restricted to the realm of the literate and remains a literary project is no longer feasible as an effective strategy for action. Argument and objective analysis, pure content, abstract thinking, logic and evidence, these forces of the word-centered world have lost their creative potential. Literate reason and the literary critic have become relics of the past. ●

With the collapse of the literary as a powerbase, the postmodern situation becomes torture for the class of intellectual elites. As dynamics change in favor of praxis and the instrumental, the engineers of academia find themselves running out of business. An age that is not centered around the idea is no longer willing to pay the price for concept-mongering. Realizing their waning power, conceptualists and idealists desperately try to produce theories of the non-conceptual, often invoking specially developed "anti-concepts." By so doing, they prove what they attempt to disprove – their own growing irrelevance.

The business of self-respecting philosophy at this turn of history is not to create or analyze conceptual abstractions. To the contrary, philosophers in the twenty-first century must create **images** of responsibility, vision and critical force.

Ours is an age of images and simulacra. Philosophy must be ready to operate within the realm of images because that is where the "real" is taking form. Since market forces produce images, philosophy must join the struggle of creating images by marketing its products through mass media, which are the supermarkets of late capitalism.

# Media philosophy

is kitsch.

The move from philosophy-as-argument to philosophy-as-literature is a Kierkegaardian leap far too frightening for Anglo-Saxon philosophers. A still more breathtaking challenge is the leap from current academic practice to **image-centered philosophy** – to imagology.

We must reinvent the art of persuasion. Argument, like print culture itself, is a privileged technology of persuasion whose authority western philosophy has taken for granted. Arguments and print still enjoy a privileged institutional status in philosophy. It is time to question the accepted paradigm of persuasion.

Media philosophy challenges the dominant view of the role of philosophy in the guerrilla warfare of contemporary culture with an openly pragmatic approach to the art of persuasion. The question concerns the status of reason in our age. Institutionally legitimated analytic reason, which is emotionally detached and socially indifferent, becomes irresponsible and immoral in an era of looming ecological disaster and global agony.

We must not only step beyond abstract arguments and essence-hunting but move from the paradigm of ideal conversation to an immersion in the dirt and confusion of non-verbal praxes. With imagology, philosophy leaves the world of print culture to enter the realm of images, simulacra, gestures and art forms. Struggle now takes place in a world where images define the field of gravitation. You become relevant through your image only if you become an artist and exploiter of the imaginary register.

In the mediatrix, you become image and thus less real. But, paradoxically, through this loss of so-called reality, you become more real than ever before.

The media as currently constituted are

preoccupied with the description and analysis of

Media philosophy attempts to move beyond existing institutions to imagine and fashion possibilities that **might be.** The challenge for the imagologist is to displace the aesthetics of despair with the politics of hope. The momentum of the moment is created by the instant in which the eternal return of the same becomes the aleatory irruption of difference.

The imagologist follows the challenge that Goethe poses at the end of **Faust**: "In the beginning was the deed." Rejecting this charge, intellectuals insist that theory must precede practice. To move too quickly, to decide without careful reflection is to act irresponsibly. But such theorizing is itself a form of practice that is often irresponsible. Goethe suggests that decision – practice, engagement – **precedes** knowledge. To know, one must first do. Throw yourself into practices and learn them from the inside out. Then and only then will you be able to theorize the processes in which you are engaged. To venture into the media is to make a blind leap. Only from such blindness does insight emerge.

# To be a media philosoph er is to be a sign painter.

**M**edia philosophy forms social sculptures rather than theories or textual products.

# Ending the Academy

In a hypertextual environment, all philosophy must be interactive. Monologue becomes dialogue or, more precisely, polylogue. The disappearance of the monological voice is a radical revolution in the history of philosophy. What usually goes unnoticed is that what has traditionally passed for dialogue is actually monologue. When monologue (even in its dialogical form) becomes impossible, classical philosophy comes to an end. But the end of traditional philosophy is not the end of philosophizing. With the death of the Philosopher, we all become philosophers with a sense for what matters. Professional philosophers remain committed to elitist culture, which dismisses low or popular culture as insignificant. Philosophers usually try to disguise this dismissal by insisting that they are developing a "commonsense" philosophy or a philosophy of the "everyday." But they are willing to accept the commonplace, the everyday, only after it has been "cleansed" by the priests of high culture who continue to rule from the cathedral of the academy. The media philosopher, by contrast, is committed to smuggling shit back into the house of thought.

Meeting at the Copenhagen airport.  Discussion of the list of topics

An innocent reader of Plato might conclude
that the task of philosophy is fourfold:

**1.**

in the face of death to provide a viewpoint and orientation
beyond the reality of this world

**2.**

to represent and elaborate morals as an existential dimension of
the human condition

**3.**

to pursue politics and the common affairs of the society with
attention to the overall scheme of things

**4.**

to conduct critical conceptual analysis

Not much of all this is left today.
What remains of philosophy when
there is no exit from the cave?

**May 31, 1992**

for the seminar and the list of readings for the students.

An artist of philosophy?  A salesman and politician, developer and visionary: what is called for in the field of philosophy is management by wondering around.

The imagologist does not seek truth but entertains enigmas.  Though in opposite ways, the academy and mass culture worship at the altar of clarity and simplicity, which the imagologist shatters.  Institutions of triviledge abhor enigmas that ought to be cultivated.

**June 17, 1992**

**Dear Esa,**

Just got back from Japan
yesterday. If there is any
country that embodies what we
are exploring in imagologies,
it is Japan. We would have
no trouble finding support
for our project there.
    It was, indeed, good to see
you briefly in Copenhagen. I
agree, everything is pretty
much in place. We should
have the link established no
later than the first week of
September. Then if there are
problems, we will have enough
time to work them out. We
should also plan a trial run
the week before our first
meeting.

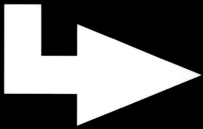

Confinement within the culture of expertise creates an arrogance that open society renders utterly transparent. Nothing is more comic than the academic trying to explain something to the public. When the masses laugh, the academy doesn't get the joke.

The imagination must be undisciplined. That is why the university cannot bear it.

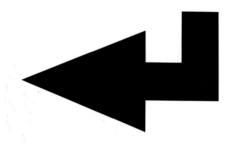

To argue for maintaining the canon in the age of telewriting is like demanding truth from television.

If the market is global, there is no such thing as foreign policy; all policy is domestic and all domesticity is economic. In so-called post-industrial capitalism, the economy realizes dimensions of human interrelation of which philosophers have dreamed for centuries. The irony is that the academy remains blind to the advent of this global community. As a result of this blindness, academics become vestigial traces of a world that will never return.

There is no such thing as American philosophy. There never has been and perhaps there never will be. Unlike America's most powerful writers, who constantly suffer the "anxiety of influence," America's "philosophers," who are never powerful, suffer the "anxiety of originality." Instead of dreading their secondary status, they revel in it. The home of truth is EUROPE and, therefore, the only philosophy that deserves the name is European philosophy. So-called American philosophy is actually a European import. Not all imports, of course, are of equal value. For the American philosophical establishment, the most treasured foreign commodity comes from England. According to most American "philosophers," the only philosophy that deserves serious attention is British analytic philosophy. The linguistic paradigm is endlessly refined but seldom questioned. The result is an orthodoxy that borders on the religious and a triviality that would be comic were it not so pathetic. To appreciate the absurdity of contemporary American "philosophy," imagine a Beckett character reading aloud from the

# Journal of Philosophy.

The triviledge
that legitimizes
the academic
critic renders
him impotent.
Merely
a Peeping Tom
who gazes from
afar but refuses
to enter the fray,
he becomes
nothing more
than a limp dick.

Problems still loom large. The connection between Helsinki and Williamstown is not yet working - for technical reasons that Finnish Telecom's Risto is trying hard to overcome. He says that the two machines should be able to speak to one another but, because they are made by different companies, there are unexpected, hard-to-define incompatibilities. Risto now says he may try to get a CLI machine and install it for the project. While it is routine to establish a contact to various locations in Europe, the US standards pose unexpected problems.

# Ending the Academy

in spite of enormous intellectual effort to gain insight into the use of language by some of the most brilliant thinkers of all time, in spite of an enormous literary effort to create new discourses by some of the most creative conceptual giants of all time, philosophy remains strangely crippled and impotent. Far from creating a single product that sells successfully in this era of communication, triviledged philosophy remains unmarketable.

Institutions of higher education have not taken advantage of the resources and energies circulating beyond

# the walls of the academy.

As a result, cultural analysis is separated from the very condition of its own possibility. To overcome the isolation

of the intellectual critic, it is necessary to enter the mainstream of culture by leaving the confines of print.

in the mediatrix, no work is a masterpiece or any work is a masterpiece. It is not simply a question of reversing high and low but of erasing the very distinction between elite and mass. Cultural conservatives cry in vain, for simcult renders the notion of an established canon passé.

Enlightenment no longer automatically sells. Nor does critical thought. To sell your product, you must get down to business and take advertising and marketing seriously. The discourses of scholarly achievement not only define the wrong agenda but have no promotional strategy. If reason is to be practical in simcult, it must be electrified.

For more than a decade, I have been attacked by conservatives for espousing notions like the death of God, the end of history, the disappearance of the self and the closure of the book. What I now realize is that the critical theory in which these notions are articulated is not advanced but is really behind the times. In cyberspace, theory is practice before it is theory: God is gone, history is over, the self is scattered and the book is exploded. The nostalgia of the conservatives is reactionary; their struggle futile. Theory must become even more radical than I ever imagined or they ever feared.

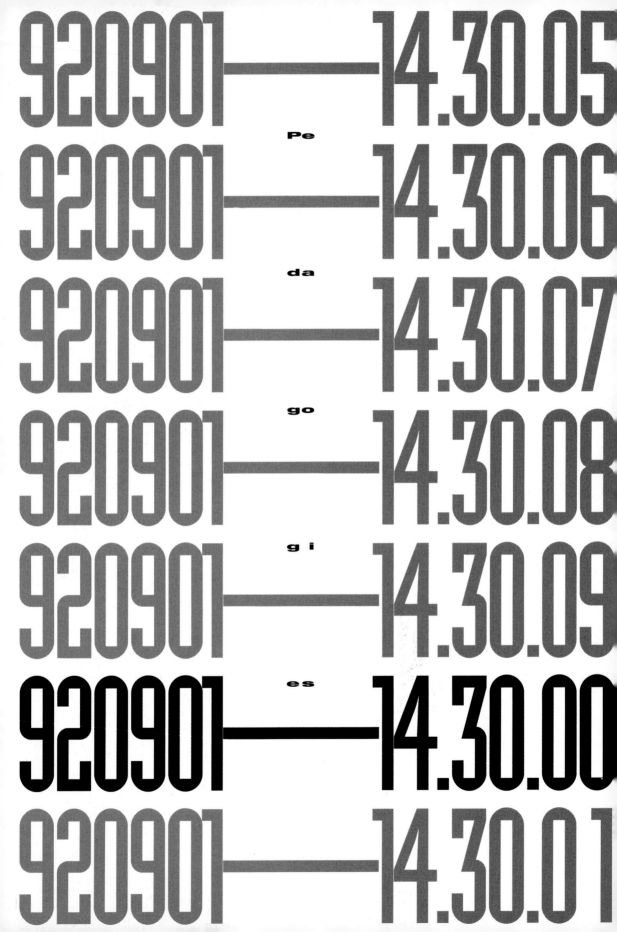

**is** communication. In contemporary society, however, education remains tied to the advancement of triviledge. The problem is not, as many suppose, the ignorance of so-called basics and unfamiliarity with the tradition. The difficulty is that the educational system is built upon structures for the production of knowledge that no longer operate effectively. The global classroom explodes the foundations of educational institutions by restructuring the space and transforming the time of teaching and learning. The master teacher is no longer a "man of letters" but becomes a purveyor of images who steals the show. The best students know how to trade purloined images.

**September 1, 1992**

**Dear Mark,**

Risto has installed a CLI machine that he borrowed from Norway, the nearest place where it was available. He has established the connection and has actually seen Mark Berman on the screen. Some problems with voice at your end, which Berman is trying to solve. Time for a trial run for us is Wednesday the 16th, 14:30 Finnish time. Everything seems set - incredibly, this project seems about to become a reality.

The modern university is a recent invention, which was initially defined in Kant's **The Conflict of the Faculties** (1798) and first realized in the University of Berlin (founded October 10, 1810). My most vivid memory of the University of Berlin dates from the fall of 1971. Having made my way to East Germany, I finally found the place where Hegel and Schleiermacher had both lectured at the height of their fame. In the main entry hall, there was a huge brown marble wall with Marx's thesis on Feuerbach emblazoned in large gold letters: "Philosophers have interpreted the world, the point is to change it." As I took out my camera to photograph this advertisement, I was seized by three security officers and thrown out. It was forbidden to take pictures inside any state-owned building.

Marx was right, the point **is** to change the world. And the part of today's world that most needs changing is the university. Kant insists that the **modern** university is an **industrial** machine whose structure mirrors the assembly line, which supports the educational apparatus. The division of knowledge into disciplines and departments is a division of labor that is supposed to increase expertise and efficiency.

But the modern university is no more suited to the postmodern world than industrial modes of production are equipped to meet the demands of electronic reproduction. To shift from the industrial to the post-industrial model for the university is to transform the modern into the postmodern university. The postmodern university will more closely resemble the decentered, disseminated and non-hierarchical "structure" of the net than the centered, segmented and hierarchical structure of the assembly line. In sum, the postmodern university is not a **uni**-versity but a **multi**-versity.

While the modern university transforms students into passive consumers who have no choice other than to accept or reject the product offered in the lecture hall, the postmodern multiversity changes students into consumers who are producers. The "place" of the postmodern university is cyberspace. No longer merely local, the university becomes global without being universal. While the universal homogenizes, the global diversifies. Within the constantly changing dataspace of the postmodern multiversity, all education is international. Conversations are not limited to one time or place but occur whenever participants can jack in. It is obvious that radically new structures and regulations will be necessary to administer the cyberversity. Old models that privilege institutional autonomy and national identity will be displaced by forms of cooperation and exchange that previously have been unimaginable.

Did not teaching change with the invention of writing?

Did not teaching change with the creation of print?

Must not teaching change with the arrival of the mediatrix?

**September 2, 1992**

Pedagogies 4

**Esa:**

   I just received word that my father died
today.  Totally unexpected.  I still am in
a state of shock and disbelief.  I'll have
to be out of touch for a week or so.  Don't
know exactly when I'll be back but will
call as soon as I can.

920902

images change the world and change us in ways that are beyond literal and linear styles of conceptualizing...

**September 12, 1992**

**Dear Esa,**

Today would have been Dad's 85th birthday. I am glad you had the chance to meet him. He really enjoyed his trip to Helsinki and often commented on your generous hospitality. From the first night with our special meal of reindeer meat and lingonberries to the final celebration of Heidi's successful dissertation, the trip was filled with memorable events.

His death this fall has cast a shadow over everything. The toughest class I ever taught was the first meeting of my Psychology of Religion course, which was held less than forty-eight hours after we buried him. I began the class by asking the students a seemingly simple question: What color is death? I have never told them why I asked that question.

As my brother and I cleaned out the attic of the house in which our parents lived for forty-three years, we were struck by the extraordinary changes their generation saw. My father was born in 1907, a mere four years after the Wright brothers' first flight. His father was born six years after the American Civil War ended. The leap from the Civil War to the twenty-first century represents a shift of worlds few will ever repeat. Flying to Helsinki was no small undertaking for a man who began his life behind a horse-drawn plow. What would he have said about our teleseminar?

Some of the concerns my father expressed in his later years stimulated my thinking about economic questions we are considering this week. Born on a farm early in this century, living through the Great Depression, and a teacher his whole life, money never came easily to him. Late in life, he collected what savings he had in an account that was overseen by a large brokerage house. He would get monthly computer printouts reporting his holdings. All of this seemed utterly unreal to him. Numbers on a page, nothing more. He frequently worried that there would be a mistake. A zero here, a zero there. How would he ever know? If there were a mistake, how would he ever prove it? Most troubling, he was never sure where his money was. I suspect his fears were not ungrounded. But, like everything else, it hardly seems to matter now.

*...To teach creatively, we must teach imaginatively.*

One of the most significant mistakes of modernists was to believe in the autonomy of culture. The insistence that culture forms a sphere apart is supposed to be a necessary presupposition of the critical function of art. Without the autonomy of culture, negative dialectics seemed impossible.

Postmodernity discloses the illusion of cultural autonomy. Culture is inextricably bound to and by the psycho-social conditions of its creation. But the denial of cultural autonomy does not necessarily imply the impossibility of critique. In the absence of any Archimedean point from which to view and criticize society, it is necessary to develop strategies of criticism that deploy available modes of production and reproduction.

If the global classroom simply replicates the structures of power that have made it possible and provides no critique of contemporary socio-political configurations, it is a failure.

**D**ay one of the Global Classroom was remarkable because it so soon became unremarkable. With my mind focussed on the dynamics of the class, and the intricacies of the texts we were discussing, I soon forgot how strange this event was. There was a moment, however, when the radicality of the situation came crashing down on me in a way that was utterly disorienting.

**Esa:** I think we need to take a look at Heidegger's argument. Let's turn to page 27.

**Mark:** What page was that?

**Esa:** Page 27.

**Mark:** OK.

Students turn to books. Pages rustle. Esa reads.

# 7hours and 7,000miles

away you are searching the "same" page as are we, as if we were sitting across the table from each other. As if? From now on, we dwell in the as if.

**A** dilemma for the postmodern teacher:

If all writing is rewriting,

then how is it possible (not) to detect plagiarism?

.

**O**ne important aspect of the conclusion of the seminar was unsatisfactory. The students resisted, even resented writing term **papers**. "What sense," they asked, "does it make to write papers for a course like this?" I insisted that the paper would provide an opportunity for them to concentrate on a particular issue and pull their thoughts together. "But concentrating on a point and pulling things together are precisely what we have been taking apart all semester."

The students are, of course, right. The teleseminar renders papers obsolete. As education becomes electronic, we will have to find other ways for students to write. It would have been more appropriate if I had pursued two of the writing experiments we built into the course. While the group poem and story we composed across the Atlantic on the net were not exactly "literary masterpieces," they did provide the opportunity to explore new ways of writing. The second experiment was less successful but no less promising. As I mentioned to you, I set up a hypertext file for the students to use in compiling their research. I required every student to record his or her notes on this file. Since every word in the text was a hot word, students could cross-reference the research of others. For example, if Jon were working on telepolitics, he could make use of Ali's research on video. This procedure made students very uneasy and initially they were reluctant to share their research. When I teach another teleseminar, I will again require students to use a hypertext research file but will extend the experiment

by asking them to write a group project for which they will all receive the same grade. The product of this effort will not be a traditional term "paper" but will be a hypertext.

The logic of communal writing follows the logic of interstanding. Electronic telecommunications technology subverts authorial property rights by creating texts whose ownership remains obscure. In this way, the net displaces the notion of the solitary creative genius that has governed our understanding of authorship for over two centuries. Letting go of the isolated author threatens the very foundation of individual identity. This threat must be embraced, for it provides remarkable opportunities for creative renewal.

What would a pedagogy for telewriting look like? For more than twenty years, I have been trying to help students write better papers. I always insist that they work out their ideas very carefully before they begin to write by outlining their argument precisely. The principles I attempt to pound into their heads are structure, order, coherence and rigor. Frequently, I tell them to imagine their argument as something like a geometric proof in which one claim follows logically from another and all taken together lead inevitably to a conclusion.

But all of these principles and strategies fall apart in telewriting. Line gives way to network to create texts whose logic is different from that of the printed page. To leave the printed page and enter the space of telewriting is to enjoy something like the return of the repressed. "Something like . . ." because this space is not the return to something we once knew but have been forced to forget; it is the advent of a different space that we have never before experienced.

Email transforms the teacher-student relationship. During our first seminar, Kaisu spoke eloquently about the way in which electronic communication enabled her to be more direct, honest and forthright than in face-to-face situations. I must confess that I was surprised by her claim and doubted its truth. I now realize she is right. Students are much more willing to approach me on the net than in person. Though I have regular office hours, students rarely come to me with their questions. In spite of my reassurances that they should feel free to call me, they are always reluctant to do so. But they do not hesitate to contact me on the net. Technology, which at first seems to create a distance by putting the machine between teacher and student, actually creates connection by bringing us together in an ongoing conversation. I have always insisted that more education takes place outside than inside the classroom. Unfortunately, the dialogue between teacher and student usually ends at the threshold of the classroom. Email erases that threshold by allowing discussion to go on any time of

# day or

A strange reversal has been working itself out in the seminar. Have you noticed how students have been using proper names? Your students seem more American than the Americans. Ignoring European protocols, they refuse to address you as "Herr Professor Doctor Saarinen" and freely call you "Esa." My students, by contrast, display none of the legendary American informality and insist on calling me "Professor Taylor." Accustomed to first-name informality, the Finnish students call me "Mark," while the Americans accept the invitation to call you "Esa." Since all of this has created a situation that is both confusing and awkward, I considered telling my students that they could feel free to use my first name, but then decided to wait to see how things developed. How long could they live with the tension between formality and informality? My little experiment did not last very long, for last week Dana broke the ice by calling me "Mark." While some students quickly followed suit, others stuck to their old ways.

I am not sure how much is at stake in this little drama. Perhaps the differences in the teacher-student relation are a function of personalities. But it is also possible that the communications technology we are using does not promote the hierarchical structuring of social relations. As the vertical becomes the lateral, the formal gives way to the informal. When this occurs, what happens to authority?

# night.

For my students in the teleseminar, your image – how you appeared when you made a point – always proves as important as any point you made. They remember your image long after they have forgotten what you tried to teach them. Contrary to the canons of Platonism, image is the medium of understanding. The pedagogical value of the techno-academic apparatus supporting our venture is relative to its capacity to generate the images that make understanding possible.

# Videovision

The home into which I was born had no TV. My memory of getting our first television is vivid – not because of my total recall but because of my father's movies. He recorded the arrival of the TV on film. In this intersection of TV and film, two epochs meet to form a site that marks a cultural shift of major proportions. .
.
.
.
.
▼

## Videovision

▼

Two things continue to impress me about my "memory" of the arrival of the television. First, the object was a luxurious piece of furniture. The mahogany cabinet was richer than almost any other furniture in our house. Indeed, in this extraordinary cabinet, the cathode ray tube seemed to disappear. I suspect this disappearance was precisely the purpose of the mahogany. In its early years, TV seemed less a familiar object than an uncanny guest invading the domestic interior. To make this invader acceptable, it had to be domesticated. The transformation of the electronic apparatus into furniture changed the strange into the familiar. Once welcomed, the guest assumed the role previously played by the family hearth. The glow of the television screen replaced the glow of the fire around which the family gathered. As the TV became more familiar, it was possible to strip away its elaborate cabinet and present it in its sheer technicity.

The second memory that lingers from those early home movies is the image of my brother, who must have been about 2 years old at the time. My father recorded my brother's first encounter with television. His reaction was extraordinary. Jumping up and down in front of the TV, he repeatedly tried to stick his finger in the mouth of the person who was singing on the screen. Though there was no sound for the movies, you could "hear" his shrieks of delight as he "touched" the "person" in front of him. In this moment, the culture of the simulacrum was born.

The televisual reflects the presence of absence that is the absence of presence.

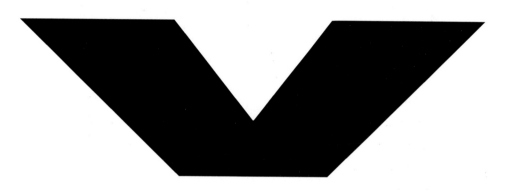

Telepresence renders visual the

wrap-around technology that has

become our milieu. In this way,

the culture of the simulacrum

realizes a specularity that

speculative philosophy could not

envision.

**Mark?**

**Esa here.**

What a trip!  This thing is really going to work after all. After months of planning and all the ups and downs, it was a remarkable moment when your image appeared.  I must admit that I was not convinced it would work until I saw you on the screen.

There are going to be some difficulties with your equipment.  Using the video cameras and mixers is not as effective as the teleconferencing equipment in our studio.  The sound is more of a problem than the image. There is an echo that must somehow be controlled.  I am sure our technicians can find a solution.

Now that I'm wired to the net, I see real possibilities for writing the book we've discussed.  Email will enable us to work in real time — while we are actually engaged in our experimental global classroom. I realize that neither of us really has time to do this now. But that is part of the point. This will be a book written for an age in which people do not have the time to write or read books.  We must try to give our readers a sense of the experience of the teleseminar and, even more important, present critical reflections on the range of topics we are discussing.  The net will allow us to achieve a level of cooperative writing that otherwise would be impossible.

The cultural logic of the remote control involves radically new syntactic and syntagmatic relations that transform not only cultural production but the very ways in which we think and speak.

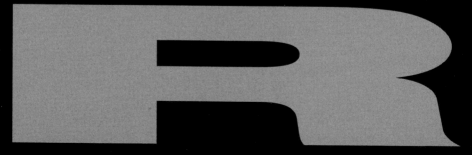

The one who controls the remote control holds the power. If the remote control governs access to the symbolic order, then it is not surprising that it is controlled by the father. The force of the symbolic order is remote control. Even when he is present, the power of the father is still exercised by remote control. The remote control is, in effect, the materialization of **le nom du pere.**

There are, of course, people who watch TV for the ads. With the help of the VCR, ad-dicks who find the programs a distraction can skip everything but the ads.

Why do boys play video

games so much more than

girls?

**W**hile critics bemoan the spread of MTV
as a more subtle but no less insidious
form of American imperialism, the rise
of global popular culture need not
impose hegemonic codes of regulation
but can open channels of communication
that allow the articulation of social
differences.

# imagologiat - satelliittiseminaari

Kyseessä on kokeileva opetusmuoto, jossa pääasiallisena opetuskielenä on englanti. Kokoontuminen keskiviikkona iltaisin klo 19-22.

**Aihepiiri:** teknisen kehityksen, erityisesti tietotekniikan ja uusiin viestintävälineisiin liittyvän kehityksen arviointi filosofisesti. Kyseessä on yritys laajentaa aikalaiskriittistä tarkastelua ajan ja paikan rikkovaan viestintäteknologiaan, uusiin representaatiotekniikoihin (esim. video) ja niiden filosofisiin seurauksiin maailmankatsomuksessamme. Keskustelu tulee olemaan filosofista eikä osallistuminen edellytä sen kummempaa tietämystä mistään bittien teknologioista.

## Seminaarin muoto:
Seminaarin johtajina ovat prof. Mark C. Taylor (Williams College) ja minä.

Yli Atlantin virittyvässä seminaarissa olemme kuva- ja ääniyhteydessä toisen aikalaiskriittisen filosofiryhmän kanssa. Keskustelemme heidän kanssaan live – tyyppisessä lähetystilanteessa ja pitkin viikkoa sähköpostin kautta. Seminaarin toteutusmuoto näin ilmentää osaltaan itse aihepiiriä ja toivottavasti avaa näkökulmia.

## Vaatimukset:
**1.** Osanottajat osallistuvat jokaiseen istuntoon.
**2.** Osanottajat esittelevät satelliittiseminaarissa kukin kerrallaan ja yhdessä jonkun amerikkalaisen opiskelijan kanssa yhden seminaarikerran aihepiirin. Tätä varten osanottajat ovat sähköpostin kautta yhteydessä Williamstowniin.
**3.** Kurssimateriaalin aktiivinen prosessointi: Joka ei ole lukenut etukäteen tarkasteltavia artikkeleita ja ole valmis sanomaan lukemastaan jotakin, lentää ulos.
**4.** Seminaaripäiväkirja – tyyppinen vapaamuotoinen loppuessee.

## Kurssin laajuus:
4 ov.
Seminaariin osallistuminen tulee vaatimaan valmisteluineen de facto 4-5 tuntia per kerta.

# imagologiat

## Kurssin sisältö:

### 23.9 Modernity and Technology

Martin Heidegger, The Question Concerning
Technology, pp. 3-35, 115-54
Esittely: Mark Taylor ja Esa Saarinen

### 30.9 Culture of the Simulacrum

Jean Baudrillard, Simulations
Esittely: Mark Taylor ja Esa Saarinen

### 7.10 Postmodernism

Fredric Jameson, Postmodernism or The Cultural Logic of Late Capitalism, pp. 1-66
Esittely: Matias Komulainen

### 14.10 Video

Jameson, Postmodernism, pp. 67-96
Sean Cubitt, Timeshift: On Video Culture, pp. 21-64
Esittely: Erkki Haapaniemi ja Ali Garbarini

### 21.10 Economy

Jameson, Postmodernism, pp. 260-78
David Harvey, The Condition of
Postmodernity, pp. 3-65, 284-307, 325-59
Esittely: Ari Tarjanne, Wayne Thomas ja Erin
Caddell

# – satelliitti–

## 28.10 America
Jean Baudrillard, America (on suom.)
Esittely: Harri Kantele ja Graham Gerst

## 4.11 Telewriting
Jay Bolter, Writing Space: The Computer, Hypertext and the History of Writing, pp. 15-31, 85-106, 121-63
Esittely: Joel Backström ja Dana Tomasino

## 11.11 Cyberwar
Paul Virilio, The Lost Dimension
........................., Pure War
Esittely: Jukka Ylitalo, Brian Malone ja Scott Miller

## 16.11 Virtual Reality
Howard Rheingold, Virtual Reality, pp. 13-46, 174-93, 378-91
Esittely: Kimmo Pentikäinen, Cynthia Llamas ja Jon Stahl

## 2.12 Media Philosophy
Esittely: Kaisu Virtanen ja Jeff Allred

# seminaari

The politics of video are ambiguous – its potential is both fascist and anarchic. On the one hand, video creates the possibility of a technology of surveillance that extends panopticism to its outer and inner limits. In a video culture the gaze is all penetrating. On the other hand, video decentralizes control by putting the camcorder in the hands of the people. When the eye of the observed turns back toward the observer, resistance becomes more than a powerless vision.

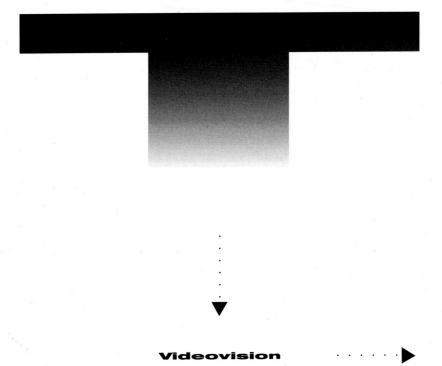

**Videovision**  · · · · · · ▶

**Dear Esa,**

"Are television and video
fundamental?  Or are they
symptoms of something deeper?"
You realize, of course, that
your question is no longer
possible.  If, as we have been
arguing, depth is but another
surface, then symptoms can never
reflect something deeper.
But your question puzzles me
in other ways.  Here in America,
where we are bombarded by dozens
of stations twenty-four hours a
day, it seems obvious that
television and video are what
once might have been labeled
"fundamental."  Simcult is, in
large part, a creation of
television.  I would, of course,
never deny that this relation is
thoroughly dialectical.  The
culture of the simulacrum
constitutes the televisual
which, in turn, determines
culture.  Nonetheless, your
question suggests that
television plays a far less
significant role in your
interpretation of our cultural
situation.
I wonder if our differences on
this point reflect the different
place of television in American
and Finnish society.  Having
lived in Europe for several
years and visited many countries
often, it has always seemed to
me that there is far less
interest in television in
Europe.  There are fewer
programs on the air for less
time.  Accordingly, people do
not watch as much TV as in
America.  Is this a significant
cultural difference?  Does it
influence the ways in which you
and I understand the culture of
the simulacrum?

HOW MANY HOURS OF TV DO **YOU**

WATCH EVERY DAY?  BE HONEST!

DON'T LIE!

## Videovision

The advent of video marks a new form of ritual activity. There seems to be something slightly illicit about viewing videos; they tend to solicit the return of the repressed by provoking thoughts and images, which, in ordinary, everyday life, are

▼

· · · · · · ▶ forbidden. In an effort to contain transgressive activity, special spaces and times

are set apart. The hour is late; doors are closed, lights turned down. Within the

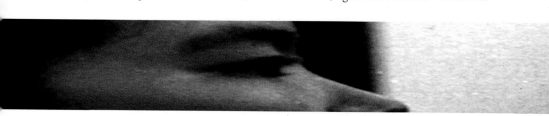

bounds of this space, time is transformed. The chronology of the quotidian gives

way to the eternal reversibility and repeatability of ritual time. Like the video

itself, ritual time can always be rewound and played again. Video-watching entails

something like a repetition compulsion that allows the expression of the forbidden.

...watching Ja...on and thinking about Hegel,

...all televangelists religious

...was a woman from the Saint-Louis Dispatch who

...the ways of televangelism are multiple;

I agree. I'll make

ort to get some of t

Televangelism

...ming.

...we will...

...existential situa...

e to new worlds we,

...the email with my time, for this

ght. For the momen...

propose we start by just writing k...

going to use the fa...

ng the fragmentary lines. We mig...

ause I have been ta...

using at this juncture to correct a...

ing some problems

...nonlinear...

...displaces meditation.

philosophical energetics.

While television has become a worldwide religion, religion has become televisual for millions. When the pulpit becomes the screen, the audience expands exponentially. Though liberals always take pride in their social responsibility and engagement, they have failed to realize the potential of electronic media. It is the religious right that has been most effective in mobilizing the resources of simcult. Through radio and television, supporters of conservative religion spread their message across the globe. But their tactics extend far beyond the airwaves. Through skillful advertising and marketing strategies, conservatives have created an extensive economic infrastructure. When the tele-preacher asks, his disciples pay. All of this is utterly paradoxical: those who are supposed to be preoccupied with other-worldly matters have become accomplished professionals in the business of this world.

In simcult, traffic in indulgences has become televisual and telephonic. Charge your ticket to heaven on Mastercard or Visa. Where is our contemporary Luther?

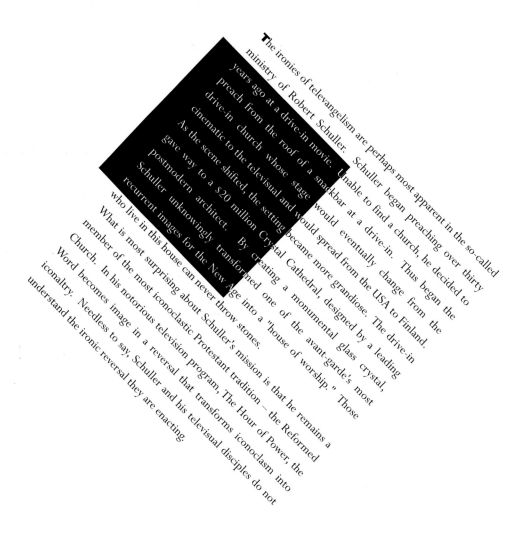

The ironies of televangelism are perhaps most apparent in the so-called ministry of Robert Schuller. Schuller began preaching over thirty years ago at a drive-in movie. Unable to find a church, he decided to preach from the roof of a snackbar at a drive-in. Thus began the drive-in church whose stage would eventually change from the cinematic to the televisual and would spread from the USA to Finland. As the scene shifted, the setting became more grandiose. The drive-in gave way to a $20 million Crystal Cathedral, designed by a leading postmodern architect. By creating a monumental glass crystal, Schuller unknowingly transformed one of the avant-garde's most recurrent images for the New Age into a "house of worship." Those who live in this house can never throw stones.

What is most surprising about Schuller's mission is that he remains a member of the most iconoclastic Protestant tradition – the Reformed Church. In his notorious television program, The Hour of Power, the Word becomes image in a reversal that transforms iconoclasm into iconaltry. Needless to say, Schuller and his televisual disciples do not understand the ironic reversal they are enacting.

If Disney World is the parodic embodiment of simcult, Heritage Park USA is its religious equivalent. The Kingdom of God made plastic!

The ways of televangelism are multiple and devious. The power of the electronic word is not limited to the TV programs of the Robertsons, Falwells, Bakkers, Swaggerts and Schullers. Religion has entered the televisual mainstream through its appropriation by politicians who try to bask in the glow of its halo effect. In search of

# Pope John Paul II has become the first television pope. He recognizes the power of the media and uses it effectively to spread conservative dogma and reactionary social gospel.

legitimacy and authority, they seek the blessing of those who wear their religion on the screen. Over the past half century, no one has had freer access to US presidents than Billy Graham. What does this TV

preacher tell presidents behind closed

doors?

Not all televangelists are American. The Ayatollah Khomeini used the media with Hollywood finesse. Indeed, the Islamic revolution would have been impossible without TV.

Resurgent fundamentalisms pose one of the most serious threats to world stability. We must not only worry about the bomb falling into the hands of terrorists. No less troublesome is the way in which religious extremists are able to control the media. Bully pulpits become much more dangerous when they are electronic.

Nor are all televangelists religious conservatives. One of the most fascinating aspects of the computer revolution is a surprising mixture of technical sophistication and mystical aspiration. The mysticism of computer freaks is not Christian. Many of the most outspoken evangelists of electronic technology have learned the lessons of eastern religions. The goal of life, they insist, is the unity of consciousness, which becomes possible on the net. Computation displaces meditation.

**E**xpressing his most profound hope for the technology he fathered, Jaron Lanier predicts that virtual reality "will bring back a sense of shared mystical altered states of reality that is so important in basically every other civilization and culture prior to big patriarchical power." In this apocalyptic vision, to don goggles and gloves is to enter an other world here and now.

## October 2, 1992

**Dear Mark,**

   For me it is a problem to get
"serious writing" done at any time.
But this is exactly why we should
grasp the moment and live through
it, in our existential situation
qua philosophers, this weird time
in history.  Maybe the email will
help me, for this medium invites a
spontaneous, sketchy approach.
   I propose we start by just
writing back and forth comments on
the themes of the seminar, along
the fragmentary lines.  We might
even force ourselves to speech-like
tactics by refusing at this
juncture to correct anything.  Aim:
a non-linear collection of
explosive, philosophical
energetics.

Electricity is an occult force that is the light of the world. This light is one, though the lamps are many.

## October 3, 1992

**Dear Esa,**

   OK, I agree.  I'll make an effort
to get some of these thoughts down
as we go along.  I am assuming,
however, that we will be able to
rework as we go along.  For the
moment, I am going to use the fax
because I have been having some
problems with the email.

While I was reading Jameson and thinking about Hegel, the phone rang. It was a woman from the

# Some of the most intelligent and

**Saint-Louis Dispatch** who wanted to ask me some questions about the recent reemergence of

# articulate preachers of the

goddess worship.

# electronic gospel proclaim a New

Do you think the return of goddess worship is a passing fad or should be

# Age in which not only omniscience

taken seriously?

# and omnipotence but, more

Both. It is a passing fad that should be taken seriously.

# important, omnipresence becomes

What could be more distant from televisual electronic revolution than goddess worship? To

# possible. In cyberspace, the

technophobic followers of the goddess, the imperative is to return to the rhythms of nature from which

# limitations of temporality and

modern culture separates us. From this point of view, the electronic domain appears to be inescapably

# spatiality seem to be overcome in

masculine. So understood, electronic technology violates nature by cutting us off from the body that

# an out-of-body experience that

nourishes us. There is, however, another way to read all of this. The mediatrix is, after all, a matrix.

# realizes the most ancient dreams of

And this matrix is the **mater** that nourishes us all. The pulses of the mediatrix are no less creative than

# religion. Fleeting electronic images

the rhythms of "mother nature."

# carry the hope of immortality.

**S**urface is no longer superficial; nor is it profound.  In simcult, the very opposition between depth and surface

must be refigured. The approach of the surface, which has been a long time coming, has not yet fully reached arrival. The erasure of depth is the inverse image of the disappearance of transcendence. Superficiality actually issues from the death of God. The death of God is not a "literal" event (whatever that might be) but can be conceived as a trope for the disappearance of any reality that is above, below, or beyond the surface of the world. To insist that the so-called real is nothing other than a play of surfaces is not to claim that surface is simple or the "real" is anything less than complex. The complexity of superficiality does not, however, involve alternative epistemological or ontological dimensions. Surfaces fold into surfaces to create convoluted structures that are infinitely diverse, constantly changing and perpetually mobile. To attempt to escape the play of surfaces is to continue the dream of western philosophy and religion. To awaken from this dream is not to suffer disillusionment but is to appreciate, perhaps for the first time, the endless potential of superficiality.

is only

skin

Reality

deep

**Dear Esa,**

I suspect our experiment was destined from the first time we met. I believe it was in the fall of 1984.  The occasion was an international Hegel conference held at the University of Helsinki. At the time, you were not only a distinguished young philosophy professor but, perhaps more important, your rock album was the rage of Finland.  Media philosophy, it seems, appeared before we knew what was happening.

For my part, the simulacrum entered the classroom while I was in Finland.  The Helsinki conference took place when Williams was starting the school year.  Thus, I had to miss the first class session of my course in the Psychology of Religion.  In an effort not to fall behind before the term began, I taped my first lecture. I asked someone to go into the class on the first day, say nothing to the students, start the tape recorder, and walk out.  The students, I was told, were initially amused and disoriented.  When they eventually realized what was going on, they opened their notebooks and diligently started taking notes as if I were present.  What was most remarkable about this experiment was that not a single student ever said anything to me about what had transpired.  Was it too ordinary or too extraordinary to mention?

superficiality²

The disappearance of depth marks the end of necessity and the release of chance. The aleatory always provokes uneasiness, even anxiety. In an effort to cope with the dread of change, underlying structures of determination, which can range from divine intention to natural law, are posited. If, however, depth is nothing more than another surface, what appears to be necessary is actually an alternative permutation of superficial chance. In the culture of the simulacrum, everything becomes chancy. The risk of the aleatory need not provoke paralyzing dread but can prove liberating for people who have had to bear the chains of necessity far too long. Within the register of the imaginary, structures of determination appear to be constructed to avoid the anxiety that freedom inevitably provokes. The challenge is to apprehend anxiety as the pulse of life rather than the mask of death.

The surface of words is the no-where where meaning vanishes.

Suppose the problem is not meaninglessness but meaning. Suppose the dilemma is not to find meaning in the midst of meaninglessness but to free ourselves from the burden of meaning. Why must everything be meaningful? Simcult opens us to the unbearable lightness of meaninglessness. To attempt to fix meaning is to try to escape the dynamic superficiality that is our vital matrix. To construct meaning is an act of repression that closes as much as it opens. To embrace meaninglessness is not to despair but to welcome the incomprehensible plurality that is our destiny.

superficiality3

The productivity of surfaces is actualized in today's software technologies. Consider, for example, the possibilities opened by Windows or equivalent programs. In the intertextuality of cyberspace, surface does not hide depth; rather windows open to other windows whose surfaces disclose other surfaces. As this technology is adapted by the telecommunications industry, unprecedented possibilities for the dissemination of information emerge. The restrictions of limited newspaper space and air time give way to a lateral extension in which topics expand without limit. For people who are interested, a simple click enables further consideration of a broad range of topics and issues. Furthermore, the passivity of traditional televisual media gives way to interactive dialogues in which the reader/listener does not simply accept what is given but asks questions and             even offers reactions and responses. Within this communications network, superficiality             allows for a "depth" that has never before been possible.

**O**ne       must       look      **at**      not   **through**  teletexts.

**N**aiveté should not be confused with superficiality. While the practice of naiveté presupposes a certain superficiality, superficiality does not necessarily lead to naive practice. The postmodern condition is inescapably superficial. If one is to act in the postmodern world, it is necessary to adopt a superficial stance. But only a person who is naive would dare to deploy superficiality. Naiveté is belief in surfaces for the sake of practice.

**i**magology is a throw-away philosophy.

**Dear Mark,**

Personally, I seldom read books.

In the midst of speed, reading a book takes too much time. Reflecting on my life for the last ten years or so, I observe that reading a book, the whole book, some serious book, is a rare and delicate event. (Like many others, I've probably read more books around airports than in my armchair.)

▶

You might say that skipping through
a book is as important an aspect of
"creative reading" as the cumbersome,
clumsy process of actually going
through a sentence.  You might say
that part of professionalism is one's
ability to sense intuitively those
parts of the textmass that are not
really worth reading, together with an
ability to concentrate on the
so-called essential.  All this is true
but does not conceal the scandal of
reading:  the fact is that the culture
of books, printing and reading remain
overwhelmingly defined by the
micropowers of non-reading.  For no
one reads that much.  A superb
bestseller might sometime win the
moment but mostly both thick and thin
books go to the bookshelf untouched.
   Professional expert cultures
legitimate their non-reading by
defining essential reading in a
limited textmass in narrowly
circumscribed forums of publication.
(The president of the Statistical
Central Bureau of Finland recently
said that all information needed for
the decision-making of this country is
published by that bureau.)  In
academia, the culture of articles,
reports and other least publishable
units will thus necessarily strengthen
itself, and fragmentary textures will
become still more fragmentary.
   The more scientists, scholars and
experts there are, the more the
culture of reading is taken over by
the culture of non-reading.  Is this
merely another aspect of the
characteristic overproduction of late
capitalism?  Is the asset of reading
declining in favor of non-reading
simply because of the overproduction
of potential reading materials?
I think more is at stake.

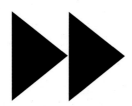

In late capitalism, **we have entered a culture of excessive refusal**, a turn-channel society, in which categories like choice, will and prioritization lose their positive force and become constituted through light-minded negativity. The result is a collapse of freely choosing subjectivity under the landslide of reified and readymade non-choices. Thus, when you choose a president, you do not vote for the person you want as the president, but against those you don't want. There is choice, but this choice is non-existent as a positive possibility. The cultural production of negative options overrides my personal production of a single choice. In the midst of that magnetizing, unending overproduction of impersonal options, my sole concern amounts to a game of light-weight crossing-outs among a domain of readymade candidates.

This means, among other things, that ours is not exactly a consumer society. We don't consume because primarily we reject. We are driven less by desires than by listlessness. We don't select a commodity by an inspired, excited, positive we free choice, a commodity that then consume, throw away, and replace with a better one. One praxis is not determined by strong positive choice but by a weak, capricious, negative rejection. Such a culture of nervous deserting opens a desert with no fresh oases in sight.

The problematics of a society of capricious deserting are particularly flagrant in print culture because every text carries innumerable marks of uncounted other texts that suggest a rejection of the first text. Should I not postpone this reading until "a better moment"? Should I not first go through some key background material? I'd love to read Goethe, but should I not wait until I start my German lessons? Books are there to be hysterically or rationally rejected. Furthermore, book culture, under the pressures of the imperatives of speed, seems to yield too low cost/benefit ratios for the conscious user the moment he or she is outside his or her field of expertise. It takes perhaps ten seconds to process a poem but you never seem to have that ten seconds available.

The result is a bewildering communal play-act. Because knowledge and insight-production remain associated with reading and the book culture, an immense joint effort is produced to maintain a façade of active reading. Insofar as media philosophy is an effort to step beyond the culture of reading, it will run counter these dominating pretensions.

Shock-effect reading - that is what I would recommend. Hypertextual reading, in the sense in which you jump around at will in a given textmass, not necessarily intending to grasp the truth, the whole truth, and nothing but the truth. Instead, you just pump gas into your engine.

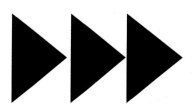

superficiality[8]

In my teaching, I've tried to use this method by xeroxing one page from a randomly chosen volume, with the intention of commenting and getting inspired by that text outside its "real" context. Excellent results, given that students don't like to read any more than I do. Once you make rejection explicit, you can concentrate intensively, at least for a moment, on a paragraph in the text.

But academic expert culture is a culture of command. You want to secure authority. You achieve command and authority by subjecting yourself to institutionally legitimated intellectual and sociological power structures. You achieve command by being yourself commanded, and you secure authority by subjecting yourself to institutional authority. And, most important, you become an object of impersonal powers of deserting. These powers indicate to you a tiny oasis of expertise in what is presented as a desert of inessentialities. You do not really desert because you are deserted. This is the message of salvation that expert culture delivers in the middle of agonies created by a culture of deserting.

You are an expert. Even when you desert, which you will do systematically, you can point to institutionally legitimated structures of intellectual expertise. You will insist that you have not really deserted the slaughters and laughters of the world of bureaucrats, the evening news, nuclear arsenals, holes in the ozone layer - the world of the trans-theoretic praxis -

but have only "put it aside temporarily," pending the conclusions of a unified science. Proudly staying behind the tightly guarded doors of your expert culture, you assume that you haven't deserted the world of concrete action and agonies but have only bracketed it. You remind yourself of essentialities and point out that the world exists only as defined in terms of disciplines, and no one can command them all. In order to concentrate on anything, everything else must be set aside.

Such are some of the canny routes of deserting in a culture of excessive rejection. The theater of pretensions returns. You pretend that you represent book culture and have convictions about the profundities founding that culture, when, in fact, your reading is mostly non-reading. You are constituted by hysterical, capricious desertion but believe you choose by conviction, based in scholarship and the intrinsic values of reason.

This result might be accepted as a hilarious, not-too-serious consequence of weak self-perception were it not for the collective disasters to which it leads. More and more of what is written is less and less relevant, not only because it deals with the irrelevant but also because fewer and fewer of us read anything relevant or irrelevant. We hardly seem to care if anything is relevant or irrelevant. With the war machine of impatient deserting gaining momentum, the first casualty is positive choice, the second is relevance.

superficiality

In simcult, we have no intellectually secure foundation for anything. And yet, we must act. This is the starting point of media philosophy: secure-in-insecurity, we cannot avoid acting in the world with priorities, a sense of relevance, and values. The kind of action in the world that we need is possible only with the category of positive choice. Under the urge to act, the media philosopher breaks with a tradition that has been strong since at least Descartes – the intellectual tradition that centers on the question of secure footing. Instead of looking for secure footing, a foundation of knowledge or a universal framework for rational discourse, the media philosopher, surrounded by insecurity, stumbles and opts for action. He opts for action also instead of elaborating, in joyfully cynical terms, the deconstruction of any secure footing.

Insecurity of means, insecurity of goals.

Insecurity of means, in opposition to the security of means of the traditional scholar, conventional rationalist, institutionalized reason. When Derrida starts up his engine of neologisms, sophistications, literary and conceptual elaborations, his staggeringly wide reading, inside the monument of French letters, inscribing his visions through writing and through the culture of books, is he not, in his own way, secure in means, as he rolls out volume after volume of commentary, heavy argumentation and histories of thought, all of which lead to his own thought, rich in abstract developments and theories?

Such security of means, embedded in print culture and in philosophy as an academic discipline inside university technologies, is not available to a philosopher who is a guest on a TV talk show or who is a performing lecturer, once he leaves the auditoriums of the academy and fires his arsenal in front of workers in a factory, managers of a commercial bank, or the staff of a hospital. Once the general public, in opposition to an expert culture, defines even part of the parameters of the communicative situation, the security of means is gone. The philosopher is left with the frightening task of creating, for that occasion, an operative vocabulary, tactics of relevance and communicative force, under the gaze of an Other, for the purposes of that Other.

Thus, in praxis-oriented media philosophy, writing and reading books lose their unquestioned status as signposts and operational forces. The stronger the urge to act, the lighter the command to follow conventional routes, even routes of capital victories in the days past. This means, among other things, that in your strategies of reading, the shock-effect approach is more acceptable than cumbersome, conventional methods.

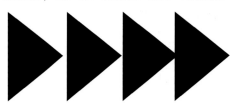

superficiality 10

The responsible postmodern intellectual will interpret these conclusions as liberation - liberation that is accompanied by solidarity. The media philosopher is alone in his undertaking; without support from others, he carries the weight of choosing his weaponry for a particular combat. The security of means, guaranteed by the academy's institutional history, is gone in the battleground of the world, the lifeworld, your personal world, the world of the media, and the world of immediate action.

The media philosopher faces the insecurity of goals. Yet, he must have goals. This is the point at which the media philosopher must not look for books or for intelligence but at his loved ones - his children fast asleep in bed. The media philosopher must penetrate with sensors of tenderness into that sleep of trust, into that breathing of hope. The conclusion will follow - radical conversion. There are no transcendent, God-given, foundational intrinsic goals, no values you can demonstrate and prove beyond all doubt. But as you open your sensitivities, no proof is necessary.

A conviction, a personal choice. Faith. Emotional, subjective truth. A postmodern Kierkegaardian leap. No technologies of desertion, not even your intelligence or the power structures of institutionalized rational thinking, can force you to break away from the essentials of that non-foundationalist, fundamental aspiration of humanity, the aspiration activated by the radicality of babies.

You embrace your babies and smell that odor of life, you crash with the world of process and concreteness head-on, with the urge to make a difference in the name of care. Love is commitment, and commitment is your urge. Who cares if you don't read all the books, most of the books, none of the books completely: the praxis of reading is but one means among others; this is an age that calls for instrumentalities to step down from their commanding status to mere means.

If you read books, justify it.

superficiality 11

is to believe that it is still possible to realize the good.   The good, as the

philosophers repeatedly remind us, is a **deeply** problematic concept.

# Of co urse! So wh What i Forget Dwell the su rface!

**P**hilosophy lacks the courage to be superficial. Superficiality is not merely a matter of knowledge but is a style of practice. The practice of superficiality carries one beyond the bounds of expert culture by crafting techniques of adaptation that have transformative effects. Superficial practice produces a bricolage that is perpetually shifting. The superficial philosopher is the rag-picker whose trash heap is the mediatrix.

# at?
# sn't?
# it!
# on

**i**f surface becomes all-encompassing, must we inevitably "go with the flow"? Not necessarily. Instead of simple acquiescence, it is possible to cultivate a stance of **critical** superficiality. This perspective accepts the unavoidability of the superficial and yet insists on the possibility of a style of criticism that deploys the very systems and structures of media culture. Something like a politics of the imaginary is beginning to emerge.

From:      IN%"SAARINEN@cc.helsinki.fi"
To:        IN%"imagologies@williams.edu
CC:
Subj:      **Telewriting**

Received: from rowe.williams.edu by
  <01GQ636JW7RK8WWXPS@WILLIAMS>; Tue,
Received: from cc.Helsinki.FI (hylka
  SMTP id AA06852 (5.65c+/IDA-1.4.4 f
  20 Oct 1992 10:44:27 -0400
Received: from hylk.Helsinki.FI by h
  <01GQ6FNNFXJW9D674S@hylk.Helsinki.F
Date: 20 Oct 1992 16:43:09 +0200 (EE
From: SAARINEN@cc.helsinki.fi
Subject:
To: imagologies@williams.edu
Message-id: <01GQ6FNNFXJY9D674S@hylk
X-Envelope-to: mtaylor
Content-type: TEXT/PLAIN; CHARSET=US
Content-transfer-encoding: 7BIT
Mime-Version: 1.0

-OCT-1992 10:42:37.83


LIAMS (PMDF #12044) id
 Oct 1992 10:42 EDT
lsinki.FI) by rowe.williams.edu with
<imagologies@williams.edu>); Tue,

.Helsinki.FI (PMDF #3241 ) id
 Tue, 20 Oct 1992 16:43:09 EET

Ours is the age of post-literacy.  How does one write for a post-literate age?  This

lsinki.FI>

II

question will remain unanswerable as long as we do not distinguish post-literacy from

illiteracy.  To be post-literate is not necessarily to be illiterate.  The illiterate cannot read

while the post-literate read otherwise.

It is time to stop bemoaning the fact that young people no longer read as we once did. Kids probably never read as much as current critics claim they did. If the young are not reading as much as we would like, the problem might be the way we are writing. Perhaps if we were to write televisually, kids would **want** to read more.

When reading becomes speedreading, essence dissolves on surfaces whose topographies are graphed by disposable maps that we choose to follow for the time being. New terrain constantly opens as maps are drawn, thrown away and redrawn.

imagology        demythologizes        the        book.

LIAMS (PMDF #12044) id
 Oct 1992 10:42 EDT
lsinki.FI) by rowe.williams.edu with
<imagologies@williams.edu>); Tue,

.Helsinki.FI (PMDF #3241 ) id
 Tue, 20 Oct 1992 16:43:09 EET

**Dear Esa,**

   There was a hint of panic in your
message last night.  The text you had
written seemed to have disappeared
and you were afraid that it had been
lost.  Since you have not yet figured
out how to print email, I have been
printing your messages in
Williamstown.  How remarkable to have
your filing and printing system 7,000
miles away from the scene of writing.
   Your panic, however, raises broader
and more interesting questions upon
which I have been reflecting.  When
writing on the net, it is not unusual
to feel a certain fear about the
location and stability of the text.
It is not clear precisely where the
written word is located.  No matter
how many times you back up a text,
you are not sure it is "there" until
it is printed in hard copy.  It is
always possible that the computer
will crash, a thunderstorm will break
out, or the electricity will fail.
Telewriting underscores the fragility
of authorship.  Even when we think we
control the text, it is never in our
possession.

T e l e
w r i t
i n g  4

Cyberspace opens a new communicative space in which messages can be exchanged at the speed of light. Within this space, the very processes of conceptualization are transformed. Writing can no longer be understood as the material translation of an immaterial concept but is always already figural. Telewriting is a writing in and with images whose materiality is immaterial.

Email calls into question the opposition and hierarchy between speech and writing. Accordingly, telewriting creates the conditions for a new form of dialogical philosophy. Without the net, it would be impossible for us to "talk" as we are now doing. Surely our dialogues are no longer Platonic; nor are they merely written. What, then, are they?

As I was writing on my computer Kaisu intervened with a program called "Talk," which enables her to write on my screen and me to write on her screen simultaneously. Funny entry, delightful. In conversing with Kaisu in this new medium, I am once again struck by the source of her strength as our computer wizard – her laughter, her humanity.

Humanistic critics of technology often lament the disappearance of the

art of letter-writing in contemporary society. With the telephone and fax at our

fingertips, letters seem to have become a thing of the past. I often detect a note of

self-interest in such criticisms, for I suspect they express the fear that future

generations of scholars will be unemployed if they have no correspondence and

manuscripts to study. But does electronic technology really displace letter-writing?

For many years, I have only rarely written letters. But now that is changing. There

has been a transformation in the postal system that suddenly revives letter-writing.

On the net, letters not only return; they proliferate. Never in my life have I written

more letters. These letters are not exactly the same as letters of the past, but fall

somewhere between pre-electronic letters and telephone conversations. Neither

precisely writing nor speech, they are a speech that is a writing and a writing that is a

speech.

# Hypertext is a televisual collage.

**Esa - -**

By extending our project from the
global classroom to the book, we
encounter paradox after paradox.  How
can we write a printed work that
reflects and embodies the criticism
of print culture our enterprise
presupposes?  If an electronic text
can be published in printed form, is
it really electronic?  The
alternative would be to give up print
and publish an electronic text.  But
the technology necessary for
accessing electronic texts is still
rather limited.  Furthermore, most of
the people we want to reach remain
committed to print.  There is no
sense preaching to the converted.
Our dilemma is that we are living at
the moment of transition from print
to electronic culture.  It is too
late for printed books and too early
for electronic texts.  Along this
boundary we must write our work.

**October 28, 1992**

T e l e
w r i t
i n g 6

Telewriting corrupts the modernist search for purity. In the worlds of hypertexts, art forms are not autonomous but overlap without end. Word, image and sound intersect in the bowels of the machine and are projected in such a way that one must read, look and hear simultaneously.

## Telewriting is imagoscription. The

texts of media philosophy are imagoscripts that are not figural translations of non-figural concepts but are imaginary inscriptions that do not presuppose the conceptual. In the media, the body becomes an image that is the text.

Color is not incidental to message. If I say the "same" words in a different tone, their meaning is transformed. Tone changes substance. I am writing this in white-on-blue but I suspect you will read it in orange-on-black. How are we to understand the true colors of our texts?

Technology never catches up with itself. I just discovered that my spell-check does not have "hypertext" in its memory bank.

A hypertext is not a closed work but an open fabric of heterogeneous traces and associations that are in a process of constant revision and supplementation. The structure of a hypertext is not fixed but is forever shifting and always mobile. The interplay of surface and depth gives way to a perpetual displacement of surfaces that is anything but superficial. Branching options multiply, menus reproduce, windows open on other windows, and screens display other screens in a lateral dispersal that disseminates rather than integrates. Hierarchy unravels in a web where top and bottom, up and down, lose consistent meaning. Everything – everywhere is middle. Instead of an organic whole, a hypertext is a rent texture whose meaning is unstable and whose boundaries are constantly changing. There is no clearly defined preestablished path through the proliferating layers of a hypertext. Though the network is shared, the course each individual follows is different. Thus, no hypertext is the product of a single author who is its creative origin or heroic architect. To the contrary, in the hypertextual network, all authorship is joint authorship and all production is co-production. Every writer is a reader and all reading is writing. While sometimes printed on a page, the medium of the hypertext is essentially electronic. Neither simply universal nor individual, general nor particular, fixed nor fluctuating, structured nor amorphous, grounded nor groundless, original nor copy, hypertextual space displays and evokes an alternative architecture.

Telewriting opens the space of the aleatory. In the absence of time for planning, reflecting and organizing, thought becomes free to roam – even to err.

T e l e
w r i t
i n g 7

**becomes**

**hyperreal.**

**Mark:**

 Last night's session on Baudrillard's **America**
was dynamite because it revealed, in the midst of
our transatlantic seminar, that cultural
differences, however difficult to define, do
exist and carry significance even in the age of
delocalization.  Perhaps this is because you
cannot be dissociated from your body and your
social history.  Nor can you escape the
bombardment of the images produced by your local
simulacrum industry.  In a sense, I am amazed to
realize how strongly even the brightest and the
most critical American students are tied to the
mythic dimensions of America.  The only remaining
superpower of our century is the only superpower
there ever has been in the image industry.
 This helps to explain the puzzlement of your
students with Baudrillard's outrageous, ironic,
poetic and extravagant description of America.
Baudrillard's book is a collection of snapshots,
self-assured and strong, superficial and
brilliant, objectifying and image-bound,
ultra-quick and bigger-than-life.  Baudrillard
treats America like America treats everything,
yet for many of your students the book seemed
something like an offense.

**October 29, 1992**

Hypertextual writing creates a semiotic blur of cross-referencing. Every word is, in principle, a hot word that is linked to endless chains of reference, which, in turn, are linked to other referential traces. Furthermore, these networks are not fixed or stable but are constantly changing and shifting. The text is no more secure than the author is authoritative.

By pushing the encyclopedic ideal to its outer limit, hypertextual networks bring its collapse.

**Hypertext**

**is                    a**

**thinkertoy**

**.**

Telewriting struggles to be less than perfectly transparent. Printed words on the page are not merely windows to ideas re-presented by the author. To the contrary, the play of the grapheme lends the surface of the text an importance it does not enjoy in printed works. Paradoxically, the dematerialization of the text on the video screen creates the possibility for the reemergence of the materiality of writing.

T e l e
w r i t
i n g     9

Does    deconstruction    theorize    hypertext    or    hypertext    literalize    deconstruction?

The ideal of a coherent text with a clear structure of beginning, middle and end reflects print technology. The electronic text is not coherent and has no obvious narrative structure. In telewriting, there is only middle, between, inter.

Derrida has finally spoken out on computers: "If there had been no computer, deconstruction could never have happened." He is, of course, wrong and certainly knows it. Nonetheless, his point is important. Deconstruction theorizes writerly practices that anticipate hypertexts. Derrida claims to write on the computer, but does he really do so? Has the computer transformed his writing or does it simply serve as a more efficient pen? His most hypertextual text  **– Glas –** was not written on a computer and nothing that he has written since that book shows the same trace of electronic technology. To move beyond Derrida, it is necessary to write differently by pushing available technology – not only computers, but also faxes, satellites, email, muses, television, video, etc.– to their limits. This will not spell the end of deconstruction but will issue in a deconstructive practice that is socially and culturally transformative. Since communications technology is always changing, the challenge of writing otherwise never ends.

In the hypertextual environment, it is impossible to deny the infinity of the signifier. Every text is the reinscription of another text, which, in turn, is the reinscription of another text. . . . In other words, hypertexts are thoroughly intertextual. In the mediatrix, critical theory becomes everyday practice.

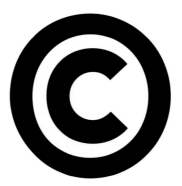

Copyright laws were formulated to regulate the exchange of the printed text. During the epoch of print, authorship and ownership were inseparably bound. Telewriting, by contrast, obscures the identity of the author. In a manner reminiscent of oral culture, the text is, in a certain sense, authorless. More precisely, the proliferation of authors elides the author's voice. In the absence of the author, it is no longer clear who owns the text.

T e l e
w r i t
i n g 10

**Dear Esa,**

A significant shift occurred in today's seminar.  With their
effort to enact telewriting, Dana and Joel entered the space of
performance.  In the exchange they staged, writing became speech as
speech became writing.  The result was a performative utterance
completely different from what past philosophers have envisioned.
The classical constantive/performative distinction, which reflects
print technology, collapses in telewriting.  In cyberspace,
performance becomes unavoidable and constantive reference
impossible.  What Dana and Joel were saying without knowing it is
that speech act theory is over.

**November 4, 1992**

**P**ost-hermeneutical reading shifts from an economy
of production (author) to an economy of
consumption (reader).  In simcult, the challenge of
writing is to write a consumable text.  Such a work
is not simply a repackaging of an older commodity
but is the creation of a different kind of text.  In this
new writing space, the author is not the sole
producer, for the consumer becomes a co-author
whose reading is a rewriting.

**A book**

for the media age must be written to be read in a
way similar to the manner in which we listen.
Writing, therefore, must become sampling and
reading lip-syncing.

T e l e
w r i t
i n g   11

In the space of

telewriting, every

reader is a flaneur who

is free to explore in a

peripatetic fashion.

Walter Benjamin would

have felt at home in the

hypertext precisely

because in this medium,

he could never feel at

home.

Unlike print technology, telewriting discourages uniformity: letters, pages, columns, spacing can be changed and modified ad infinitum. Writing and design are no longer separate activities but become different moments in a single creative process. Grapheme and icon enter into an entirely new relationship. In textual play, writing becomes drawing and painting, and drawing and painting become scripture.

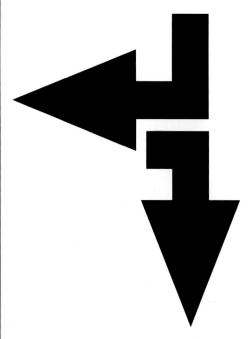

I fantasize about writing an essay on the changing technology of erasing. As writing instruments change from chisel, stylus, pen and pencil to typewriter, punch card, word processor and "mystic" pad, the means of erasing are transformed. In this case, "progress" is easy to chart. As technology improves, the trace of erasure becomes even more invisible. What is left when electronic writing is erased? It is precisely the perfection of electronic erasure that makes this form of script so unsettling.

 MARCEL
Design
Timo Sarpaneva

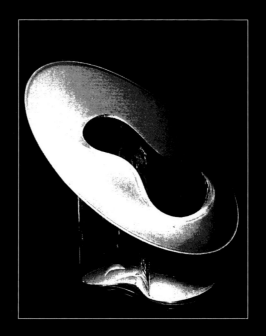

In simcult, ad diction is crafted to create addiction. Image produces desires that are necessary to keep the economy running. In the electronomy, all investments are libidinal.

## Ad-Diction

Society is something like a cybernetic system that is ruled by various governors. One of the most important regulating mechanisms is the advertising industry. Advertisements function like templates that control psycho-social processes by channelling energy and guiding activity. Regimentation by advertising becomes more extensive as the electronic means of reproduction become more subtle. The most effective ad is the one that is not recognized as such. In the culture of the simulacrum, ad-diction knows no bounds.

In simcult, it is impossible to enforce truth in advertising laws, because the warning label might be a simulation.

The logic of desire is illogical. Enough is never enough and more never satisfies. The technologies of electronic reproduction instill desires that can never be satisfied. Though no one needs to upgrade, everyone wants to do so. Who really doubts that some day there will be Word Perfect 99.9?

The image is the hallucinatory production of perception.

images are addictive; once hooked, it is hard to kick the habit.

The ad-dict buys images not things.

Hallucinogenic drugs . . . electronics . . . all-at-onceness . . .

all-at-oneness.  Fibers link these disparate points.  Virtual

reality is the LSD of the electronic age.

marimekko®

Ad-Diction [5]

**A d - D i c t i o n** [6]

**T**ransferring hope from a psychedelic to a technological revolution, Timothy Leary preaches: "Turn On.    Boot Up. Download."

**S**peed is also a drug. But not all drugs are narcotics.    Chemical prostheses can intensify experience and open the doors of perception. Travelling at the speed of light through marvelous virtual worlds sharpens perception and unleashes the imagination.

**T**he net is something of a narcotic.   It is addictive – terribly addictive.
Surely it is possible to O.D. on the net.

### Dear Mark,

Remarkable session yesterday.
Joel put his finger on a key point when he asked what are the criteria of success for a media philosopher.  If a media philosopher becomes a celebrity, isn't his or her enterprise dangerously close to ego-tripping with no further serious consequences?
Nobody can enter the media except through the magnetism of the image of his or her personality.  In media, personality, or the appearance of personality, is renewed again and again until it becomes an instrument without which success is impossible.

But personality-as-media-product is only **instrumentally** justifiable if it becomes a vehicle for change and emancipation. Using an instrument (media), you create a personal instrument (yourself as a media figure). The problem is that there is no institutional status, no established, cultural status for the realm of public discourse in the media. Public discourse is usually viewed as serving more established, institutional and elevated realms of culture. Thus, a contribution to public discourse in the media is guilty until proven innocent. If you only pursue the interests of legitimate, established discourses, your media publicity might be acceptable. As a politician, you will get away with an appearance on a talk show if you discuss education policies, and as an academic if you effectively "popularize" matters of scholarly significance. The more obvious the connection with discourses, otherwise deemed legitimate, the better your shelter. To identify forms of shelter, the media comes with product labels like "documentary," "entertainment," "current affairs," "news," etc. The crucial point to observe is that there is no product label for the public use of reason.   **Ad-Diction** 7 This means that criteria for evaluating contributions in this realm will be subjected to either arbitrary subjectivism or vested political and economic interests.

   The unpredictability of response is one important reason for the reluctance of intellectuals to intervene in the media. If you publish an article in the leading journal in your discipline, your arguments and conclusions can be challenged but your seriousness cannot be doubted. A media product, by contrast, appears frivolous and would never be characterized as "the public use of reason." Disciples of classical reason want a code of honor established in advance. If you break this code, you cannot expect to be taken seriously. If you transgress, you quickly discover that in the media you never produce just one product but always create many. The agonizing and exciting result is that you never have total product control. I remember once appearing on a Saturday-night primetime talk show, where I spoke of philosophy, my love for Pipsa, and political questions. Not everyone interpreted this appearance as the public use of reason even though I spoke explicitly about it. Perhaps this was because I wore yellow Mickey Mouse shoes and a matching silk shirt.

   A media product is ultimately constituted by others. Associations run wild, irrationality flares up, and inner forces break out. So much happens during a single media intervention. To be a media figure is to be the object of uncontrolled emotions, projected on you with ridiculous self-assurance by
                    complete strangers. ▶

But a work of art, like a novel, is also constituted
by the reader, on the basis of an incomplete version
provided by the author.  Is the media-interventionist's
fate any worse?  Yes.  The key difference is that before
the act of reading begins, the book is presented to the
reader as a particular kind of cultural product with
sophisticated, refined institutional backing.  Such
backing, at this juncture in history, is not available to
media philosophers.  Without institutional support to make
their effort comprehensible within the context of a grand
cultural project, media philosophers are at the mercy of
spitting accusations concerning the goals of their
project.
 He is a narcissist who is out there only to promote
himself.  She is a lens louse, who values only herself.
With the aim of becoming famous for being famous, they are
on an ultimate ego-trip.  When the realm of goals is
ill-defined - and the goals will remain ill-defined within
the prevailing paradigm of the serious use of reason -
instruments (i.e.celebrity status, media attraction) are
mistaken for ends-in-themselves.  Thus, a media

philosopher amounts to a person who is
contingently a philosopher by training and profession and
yet is weird enough to indulge in media orgies.
 This is my condition in Finnish society and this
condition is one of disgrace.  While traditional academic
philosophy can always claim the merit of its lofty goal,
"love of wisdom," there is no such recourse open to the
philosopher who is exposed in gossip columns and on
magazine stands in supermarkets.  And yet, this condition
of disgrace is positively exciting, for it opens a new
dimension of forceful dynamics that creates new
possibilities for philosophy.  By subjecting himself to a
condition of disgrace, the media philosopher smuggles
philosophy into the realm of relevance and the everyday.
This means, among other things, that a media philosopher
must be conscious of herself as a product and yet sustain
processes of critical thought.  Personality is nothing but
a means.  Because traditional thinking - and its ties to
print culture reenforce this - is fundamentally
product-oriented, the process-constitution of media
philosophy will not fit into the categories of evaluation
established by conventional rational culture.  It remains
unclear whether the contribution of a media philosopher is
anything other than a carnivalistic outburst of laughter.
 In short, Joel's question cannot be answered.  The
criteria to measure the success or failure of media
philosophy do not yet exist.  The charge of an
intentionally built personality cult always seems
justified to philosophers who lurk in the shadows with
flashlights.  Such judgments should not, however, be
discouraging, for other things are more urgent and more
significant.  For the transgressor, disgrace is beautiful.

**V**irtuality makes ecstasy

real.

**C**ellular phones and portable computers are the pills we pop.

**T**he white powder of the philosopher's stone has taken many forms whose traces can be detected in Acid, Angel Dust, Ecstasy, and especially Speed. When the dose is right or the charge is sufficient, Speed breaks the chains of time and space.

**T**he distance between Haight Ashbury and Silicon Valley is not as great as it initially appears. The counter-culture's technophobia always harbored a technophilia that promised to transform the chemico-religious prosthesis into the electronic prosthesis.

**T**he transition from the religious, to the chemical, to the electronic fix extends the process of sublimation in which matter becomes increasingly rarefied or idealized and thus appears ever lighter until it is nothing other than light itself. To get high on light, you don't need to inhale.

**W**ith the explosion of our email conversation, my computer has taken on a different aspect that is completely uncanny. I now know that the machine is always awake. It is like a pulsating heart, connected to the entire world by arteries and veins, and a brain that never sleeps, which is linked to other restless brains all over the globe. Though it seems to be doing nothing, the machine is quietly accumulating stuff.

# GUGGENHEIM

MUSEUM Ad-Diction[11]

Interstanding

**W**hen depth gives way to surface,
under-standing becomes inter
-standing. To comprehend
is no longer to grasp
what lies **beneath**
but to glimpse
what lies

**between.** *interstanding.*

**U**nderstanding has become impossible

because nothing stands under.

Interstanding has become

unavoidable because

everything stands

between.

Compu-telecommunications technology involves an epistemological shift no less radical than Kant's Copernican revolution. The very forms through which we perceive and categories with which we think are transformed by the changing technologies of knowledge production. Things give way to events, identities to differences, and substances to relations. Everything is simultaneously interconnected and in flux.

Episstemology offers no relief if it is not humanly wired.

**Dear Mark,**

The email part of the seminar is now gaining a momentum I had hardly anticipated. Seducing the students to rely on their intuitions, the net becomes a way of liberating the instinctual in their thinking. As the spontaneous takes the lead, we are overloaded with insights and proposals. I continue to be impressed by the quality of the stuff the students produce. Not to mention the quantity. Today when I logged in, there were no less than thirty-two messages from the students waiting for me.

It is clear now that it was vital to combine the seminar, with its intense live studio set-up, with the possibilities created by email. The relative slowness of the transmission of sound and visual image kills the chance for rapid dialogue back and forth. It forces one to listen; I have seldom listened so intensively as during this seminar. But the intensity of listening brings with it an urge for self-expression that the free-wheeling world of email can satisfy. You can allow yourself the privilege of listening carefully because you know that any point can be developed later through email. This is probably one reason why everyone takes notes like mad in this seminar.

**November 6, 1992**

Mediaeducated intui

For imagologists, textuality emerges in force fields that disrupt traditional thinking.

To deinstitutionalize the imagination, institutionalize institutional reason.

Telelogic subverts the institutions of triviledge established by expert culture. Analysis divides to conquer. Its "victory," however, is pyrrhic, for its touch turns everything into a corpse. Telelogic is an electric shock treatment whose jolt revives thought by creating live wires.

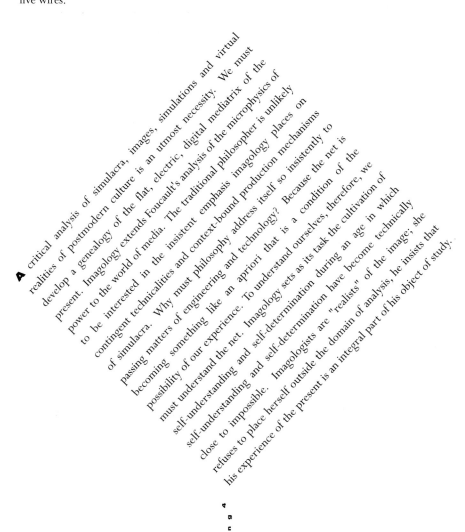

A critical analysis of simulacra, images, simulations and virtual realities of postmodern culture is an utmost necessity. We must develop a genealogy of the flat, electric, digital mediatrix of the present. Imagology extends Foucault's analysis of the microphysics of power to the world of media. The traditional philosopher is unlikely to be interested in the insistent emphasis imagology places on contingent technicalities and context-bound production mechanisms of simulacra. Why must philosophy address itself so insistently to passing matters of engineering and technology? Because the net is becoming something like an apriori that is a condition of the possibility of our experience. To understand ourselves, therefore, we must understand the net. Imagology sets as its task the cultivation of self-understanding and self-determination during an age in which self-understanding and self-determination have become technically close to impossible. Imagologists are "realists" of the image; she refuses to place herself outside the domain of analysis, he insists that his experience of the present is an integral part of his object of study.

The logic of the net is not linear or causal but associative and aleatory. Chance

**anding**

connections displace necessary relations. The shift to aleatory association is the function

of three features of net work. First, the memory capacity of computers puts at one's

fingertips quantities of data that far exceed the comprehension of any individual. When

plugged into data banks, we know far more than we can ever know we know. With a few

keystrokes, connections we never would have discovered on our own suddenly appear on

the screen. Second, the net links us with people throughout the globe who contribute

to our work in unexpected ways. When a document is sent out over the net, it comes

back modified, perhaps even transformed. The text, which is no longer my own,

becomes the source of unexpected surprise and unanticipated pleasure. Third, when the

microphone is no longer locally wired, strange echoes occur.

Though all experience is mediated, the technologies of mediation are always changing. The challenge is to explore and transform the channels of mediation. Turn on, tune in. There is no dropping out.

By erasing the boundaries between interiority and exteriority as well as depth and surface, simcult opens every closet. Though an undeniable invasion, this coming-out party also makes possible a certain "gay science."

In hypertext, all the border guards have been assassinated. The entire world of knowledge becomes a free-trade zone. In this common market, currency is current.

The circle of reproduction: knowledge produces technologies that produce knowledge.

Technologies come first, praxis comes second, theories come third. As a result of this immense shift, the site of critical thought must be redefined. We have to face the fact that the celebrated, literate techniques of critique, analysis and insight-production, together with the institutional structures that embody them, receive no applause in the theater of simulacra.

Effective human conduct surely requires knowledge. But as much as knowledge, it requires management skill and command of context. Management is the art of organizing the functioning of various compartments and departments into workable relations. Creative action in this realm requires sensibility, courage to establish priorities, the ability to weigh the relative merits of contradictory forces, the awareness of the specifics of the context, and the capacity to proceed under the conditions of fundamental uncertainty. Such creative management is needed in our cognitive realm, and, once introduced, it will revolutionize the functionings of Insight-Production Inc.

# anding

Under the old Board of Directors, Insight-Production Inc. sticks faithfully to its traditionally rigid, compartmentalized and dichotomized, organizational structure: theory vs. praxis, university vs. polytechnic, science vs. art, fact vs. fiction, fact vs. value, real vs. unreal, etc., etc., etc. However tiny his domain, the expert can always shrink his thinking still further. This is what the directors call discipline. Never questioning existing disciplinary management, the prisoner-of-expertise is happy to deliver ever more impressive trivialities to the select few. In this way, institutions, theories and attitudes stand firm. But technologies eventually shatter this firmness. As communication becomes superbly fast, cheap and spontaneous, conventional institutions of organized rational thought imprisoned in cell-like structures are condemned by their inability to function effectively. Media philosophy is based on the observation that the breakthrough in telecommunication technologies changes the very way we apprehend the world by remaking the institutions that produce perception.

Management of oneself as a synthetic-analytic-critical force in the age of media requires a fresh look at the art, technologies and politics of communication. The thinking subject must be redefined. This redefinition will force to the surface the characteristic features of the tactics deployed in managing sensibilities. Perception, thought, taste, common sense, instinctual touch, all change as the Lebenswelt shifts from the assembly line of Fordism to the net of telecommunications. When production is no longer based on the division of labor, new possibilities of synthesis suddenly become feasible.

A culture centered
on knowledge cannot
get inside its own skin. Nor can
it ever touch an other.

## There are

## no facts

## but only

## factoids

Interstanding is relational but not
dialectical, connective but not synthetic,
associative but not unitive. The between of
the "inter" neither fragments nor totalizes.

interstanding

**November 7, 1992**

**Dear Mark,**

   How did this wild project ever get going in the first place?  I
think because we are both convinced of the importance of forging a
relation between philosophy and non-philosophy.
   Your relation to Scandinavia, of course, runs deep and is getting
deeper.  Perhaps it is the influence of Kierkegaard that makes your
work resonate here in Finland.  Even when writing scholarly monographs
on classical philosophers, it was clear to me that you rejected expert
culture.  That has become obvious to everyone as you have moved from
philosophy and theology to literary criticism, art, architecture and,
now, cultural diagnostics.  In this country, the effort to relate
insights from different disciplines is what intellectual work is all
about.  This is why your work is having a growing impact both within
and beyond the walls of the academy here in Finland.
   More lies ahead.  Push on.

**W**hen truth dies, a new realm of creative expression opens for
those who refuse to believe in ghosts.

**i**n the mediatrix, identity is no longer critical but becomes
diacritical. To be is to be related and to be related is to be
plugged in.

**T**elecommunications transform the technologies of criticism.
As privacy on the page gives way to the exposure on the net,
critique all too often becomes an attack to which there is no
possibility of responding. In a curious way, the more ephemeral
the criticism, the more devastating it seems.

understanding interrupt

is the problem the absence of the community or that we do not appreciate the importance of the new forms of community arising in our midst? Telecommunications technology transforms the very conditions of the possibility of community. In the mediatrix, we are no less related for being worlds apart. The local becomes global without being universalized. Our teleseminar exceeds the bounds of the classroom by creating a virtual community that is vital.

in the community of nations, there is no standing without interstanding.

interstanding 10

interstanding   only   works         when   it   networks.

**November 8, 1992**


**Dear Esa,**

There was a hint of anxiety in your voice yesterday.  It was a tone
that I could not have heard on the net.  There are, after all,
differences between the telephonic and the teletextual.  Some things
can be heard but not read even as some things can be read but not
heard.

The anxiety concerned the problem of writing itself.  In ways I had
not appreciated, it appears that writing has become problematic for
you.  These difficulties, it seems, arise from your sophisticated
grasp of the disparity between our contemporary situation and the
philosophical tradition in which you were trained and to which, in
some sense, you remain committed.  If we are in a media age that is
truly revolutionary, then is it any longer possible to philosophize?

The depth of this problem was driven home to me the day before we
spoke.  On Saturday, I went to Boston to participate in the annual
meeting of the Society for Phenomenology and Existential Philosophy
(SPEP).  Long ago, I stopped attending the meetings of the American
Philosophical Association.  Members of the APA are, for the most part,
so hopelessly mired in the tradition of analytic philosophy that their
work has lost all contemporary relevance.  For many years, SPEP has
offered a creative alternative by keeping alive discussion of the
continental tradition.  However, as I listened to the papers and
debates last Saturday, everything seemed stuck in a time warp.  Surely
thinkers like Heidegger, Husserl and Levinas remain important.  But
the abiding significance of their work can only emerge in and through
a creative dialogue with our contemporary situation.  It is precisely
the absence of any appreciation for the significance of the changes
taking place around us that characterizes today's philosophical
discussions.

Does this mean that philosophy has become impossible?  This is the
question I hear in your anxiety about writing.  In one sense,
philosophy has indeed become impossible and we should let go of the
classical tradition without any regrets.  But in giving up a mode of
philosophical discourse that is no longer possible, we become open to
new opportunities for reflection.  It is these opportunities that we
are called to seize here and now.

You are beginning to believe that our electronic dialogue might
displace the Platonic and Socratic dialogues of the past.
Now you must act on that belief.
Take up your keyboard and write!

**V**irtual communities are as real as it gets in cyberspace.

**T**he net creates and recreates strange relations. When I was an undergraduate at Wesleyan, a student named John Barlow was in the class behind me. Since we were both religion majors, we were in several classes together. Those were the days when there was great interest in non-western religions. John was an extraordinarily talented poet who became fascinated by eastern religions. While he turned East, I turned West and our paths separated. Last spring when I began reading MONDO 2000, I discovered a John Perry Barlow who had some very interesting and important things to say about electronic technology. A few days after reading Barlow's reflections, a student said that he heard I had gone to school with John Barlow. He asked me if I knew who he was and I replied that I had lost track of him. The student informed me that the John Barlow I knew at Wesleyan was the same John Barlow who writes for MONDO. When not preoccupied with technology, John Perry Barlow is a lyricist for **The Grateful Dead.**

Several weeks ago, I came across Barlow's address in a book on virtual reality. Last spring I wrote a paper on telecommunications technology that I thought would interest John so I sent him a copy but never received a reply. As if to remind me that the virtual is not always the real, I later discovered that the address was incorrect. Then someone told me that John is on the net. Late last night I sent him a message asking him if he would like to come to Williams to talk about electronic technology. By 6:00 a.m., John had replied that he would be delighted to visit the campus.

We are now living in a different post-age. One system breaks down and is replaced by another system. With the new system, new possibilities emerge.

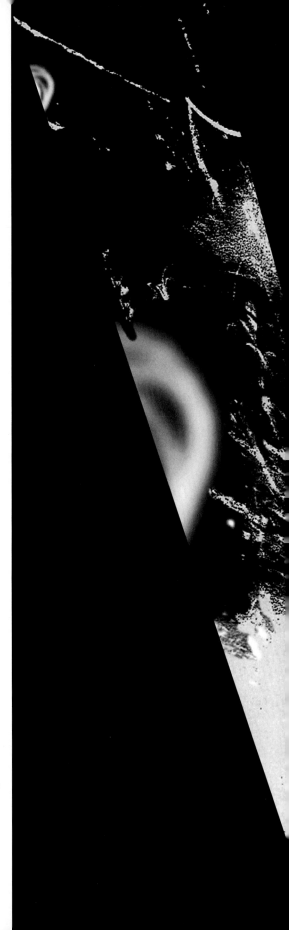

interstanding is the last hope for simcult.

A
B
C
D
E
F
G
H
I
J
K
L
M
N
O
P
Q
R
S
T

**Netropolis**

The modern metropolis is being displaced by the postmodern netropolis.

I have now two phone lines coming to my house, two coming to my studio, a fax, a university number and an email address, a pocket-size portable phone and a mobile phone in my car. Everyone says it's impossible to get hold of me.

Akihabara at night: circulation, endless circulation, relentless circulation. Circulation that seems to come from and lead nowhere. Vertical, horizontal, lateral. On the streets, on the walls, in the air. Circulation without a heart, circulation without a center – or with ten, twelve, perhaps more centers. Akihabara is a city within a city. The same pulse beats simultaneously in Shinjuku, Ginza, Ueno, Shitamachi, Shibuya, Roppongi, and elsewhere. Though nothing is disorderly, a riot is always under way. A riot of signs – audio and visual signs create a dizzying sensuous cacophony. Incomprehensible images and unreadable signs flash everywhere. Brilliant, gaudy neon colors of electric signs contrast sharply with the muted black and white of the cars and clothes of the mobs that circumambulate at the feet of these latter-day icons. The noise becomes a mesmerizing din that approaches a ritualized murmur.

Akihabara, one of the most vital commercial districts in Tokyo, has the largest concentration of electrical and electronic stores in the world. The street is an open arcade, a frenzied bazaar. Interiority and exteriority fold into each other to create surfaces that know no depth and yet are not merely superficial. Walls become screens that unveil nothing but other screens. Hundreds, perhaps thousands of tiny shops and large stores display an incomprehensible array of the latest electronic devices and consumer goods. Everything seems to be running, nothing standing still. Relentlessly bombarded by images, all is drawn into the play of signs until every substance becomes unbearably light. Everywhere I turn, I see my image projected on flat screens. Cameras I cannot locate expose me to angles of vision I have never before glimpsed. This is the society of spectacle run wild. If Japan is "the empire of signs," the emperor seems to be the signs and images that reflect only themselves. When compared with Akihabara, Las Vegas is a small town from an earlier epoch. Akihabara is the future that already is almost in our midst. We must learn the lessons it can teach us.

The space of the netropolis is cyberspace.

It is not enough to say that modernism is an urban phenomenon and postmodernism is a suburban phenomenon. What emerges with the spread of cyberspace is a social construction that is neither urban nor suburban. The mediatrix creates a simcit in which the very conditions of spatiality and temporality are transformed.

**Netropolis**

The netropolis: decentralized, non-hierarchical,

locally empowered – if you can pay for the juice.


Is the net a city without walls or do walls merely

take new forms?

The netropolis is nowhere and yet it exists.

In the netropolis, it is possible to move without changing your address. People can find you even though they have no idea where you are.

The desynchronization of local schedules creates the possibility of the synchronization of international schedules. When wired, a person can work or even teach a class simultaneously in New York, Helsinki and Tokyo while living in the remote mountains of Massachusetts.

The spatio-temporal dispersal brought about by electronic technology creates an infinite nomadism that is not necessarily a condition of exile. Though homecoming no longer seems possible, homelessness is not inescapable. The site of dwelling shifts and floats as freely as the network that is its enabling condition. Suspended in an immaterial web whose reach exceeds our grasp, all action becomes action-at-a-distance. By creating the actual conditions of interconnection about which philosophers have only speculated, the global electronic network amplifies every action on the stage of world history.

In the simcit, smaller (not bigger) is better. The grand dream is to miniaturize until you are able to hold the world in the palm of your hand.

When we "go out" while staying at home, home is no longer home but is **unheimlich.**

In the netropolis, architecture becomes electrotecture. Electrotecture surpasses the techniques of computer-aided design by actually taking responsibility for fashioning cyberspace. If we increasingly dwell in cyberspace, the architect must find ways to design the electronic environment. There is no clear line separating the electrotect from either the imagologist or the computer programmer. In the netropolis, images and programs are no longer preliminary models that are the prelude to "real" building but constitute the living space for global villagers.

Modernism involves a progressive abstraction or

..........dematerialization that presupposes what Paul Virilio aptly describes as an "aesthetics of disappearance" in which reality is disclosed as always having been essentially immaterial. When the real is believed to be ideal, sensuousness and materiality are regarded as superficial appearances concealing deeper patterns that define truth and reality. For abstract and non-objective painting as well as high modern or International Style architecture, the real is identified with abstract form or formal structure. Accordingly, the artistic and architectural task becomes the re-presentation of essential structure in aesthetic form. In this "higher" realism, which is insistently non-representational, the dematerialized object of production effectively depicts a reality that has become surreal.

Netropolis

**A**bove the parking lot for the residential complex in Okawabata Rivercity 21, a massive oval object (16 meters x 8 meters) rotates slowly. Covered with hundreds of aluminum panels, this strange construction shines brightly silver as it reflects the sunlight. At night its appearance is completely transformed. Five liquid crystal projectors inside the object transmit images on two translucent screens and on the surface panels. The images are controlled by a computer that alters lighting patterns and combines figures from five sources. As people walk beneath this floating object, they pause long enough to glimpse a fleeting image or passing bit of information. Neither a television nor video screen, neither neon nor electric sign, the layered surfaces of this televisual space project a simulated environment fabricated from the information that fills the air.

**Netropolis**

**A**s the reflection and embodiment of simcult, the simcit will be neither the utopia of modernists or postmodernists nor the dystopia of their critics but will be something else, something other, something as yet incomprehensible and unknown. The impossible task of electrotecture is to welcome this disruptive other by sponsoring endless construction, deconstruction and reconstruction.

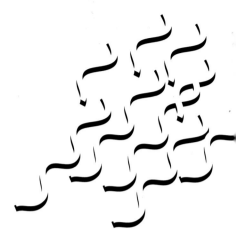

Infinitely permeable and completely iterable, the mediatrix spatializes and temporalizes without being either place-bound or time-bound. Its place is anywhere, which is neither everywhere nor nowhere; its time is anytime, which is neither ephemeral nor eternal. While the space-time of the grid is a representation of the typographic space of the book, the space-time of the network is the reinscription of the spacing of the hypertext.

How   can   you   lock   your   doors   when   you   live   in   cyberspace?

**W**hat the flâneur is to modernism, the cyberstroller is to postmodernism.

## November 8, 1992

## Dear Mark,

The reason I gave up writing academic philosophy almost ten years ago was complete frustration with philosophy as an expert culture aiming at 20-page articles in specialized journals. I was at that time editing such a journal, one of the best - **Synthese**, published in Holland - as I had done since the mid-1970's. Though I had respect for the effort, intelligence and energy of these academics struggling to straighten out some argument in someone else's contribution, I could not motivate myself to write such articles.

My disillusionment with academic philosophy coincided with deeper involvement in Finnish society and culture. Around 1980, I had started to intervene in this country, through the mass media. At that time Jan Blomstedt and I published a book entitled **Punk-Academy**, in which we fiercely attacked those we labeled the "old farts of the literary establishment." It was a pretty outrageous book that we modeled on punk rock, which at the time was a major cultural force of change in this country. This book, some related writings, and accompanying interviews in the media, created an incredible outrage in cultural circles and the literary establishment.

I remember my suspicion when the first journalist from a women's magazine called me. Can a university teacher, a self-respecting academic, appear in a women's magazine? The journalist argued that no other genre of the press publishes more on new books than the women's magazines. We met, the article came out, and now some people say they cannot open a women's magazine without there being something - at least in the gossip section - about the most photographed philosopher in this country. By the end of the 1980s, I had become a cult person and media celebrity to such an extent that when our twin boys were born in April 1989, the largest evening paper in Finland ran the headline "Esa and Pipsa: Twin Boys!" It was the leading news story in Finland that day. Through all of this, however, no clear metatheory of what I called "unclean philosophy" emerged. I had no precise conception of a project I vaguely thought of as "situational, intervening" philosophy.

Things got even crazier after the publication of **Muutostekijä**, a book on business and culture. Companies and organizations in Finland started calling and faxing to invite me to give lectures on creativity, leadership and "key challenges of the 90s." Through all of this, I have become even more frustrated with the whole discourse of the university.

Before you and I started our project of media philosophy - as an effort to break down the barriers separating technology and the academy, thinking and dialogue, superficiality and profundity, teacher and student, speaking and writing, theory and praxis -. I thought my problems with philosophy as an expert culture were idiosyncratic. Now I realize that the challenge of media philosophy defines our age. If we are to deal with the frightening prospects facing us at the end of the millennium, we must overcome immense trivialization of critical thinking. The project of media philosophy is the effort to revive and recharge philosophy, with morality and emotion. Media philosophy is philosophy in the open, philosophy in front of the gaze of anybody, philosophy whose aim is to regenerate everybody.

The netropolis becomes inhabitable as a simcit, which is completely unreal.

In the simcit, electronic mobility displaces auto mobility.

There are no citizens in the simcit — only passengers. Everyone is in transit without a final destination. Life becomes **Leben ohne warum**.

In simcit, the public square reappears on the private screen.

# Why hasn't anyone written a telephone book for the netropolis?

Electronomics

**w**here is your money now?

In cyberspace.

Where is cyberspace?

**A**aron, my son, triggered my reflection on many of the economic questions we are pursuing. The day after the 1987 stock market crash, we were talking about the extraordinary sums of money that were lost in a few hours. With all of the innocence and insight of youth, Aaron asked:

"Well, where did the money go?"

I had no good answer for his question and still am uncertain how to respond. I suppose I would have to say that the money never existed in the first place. The deeper question is whether money ever exists. What, after all, is money in simcult?

# st
# modernism's

**P** preoccupation with difference cannot be understood apart from shifts in manufacturing methods and strategies. In spite of their important differences, there is no radical break between industrial production and post-industrial reproduction. The interface of computer and machine transforms the very nature of manufacturing and, by so doing, changes not only working conditions but also the structure of social relations.

The industrial revolution was brought about by the application of the principles of Fordism to a broad spectrum of industries. The two foundations of Fordism are abstraction and homogenization. Products and tasks are standardized thereby making mechanical parts as well as workers interchangeable elements in the assembly-line process. The shift from a craft economy to an economy based on mass production required the development of mass-marketing techniques. Thus, the advertising industry emerged to create desire for standardized products. Within this climate of production and consumption, everyone seeks the lowest common denominator by trying to keep up with the Joneses.

It is important to realize that though Fordism originated in a capitalist environment, its principles have also been applied in socialist societies. The former Soviet Union extended standardization and homogenization beyond what even the most ardent Fordist dreamed possible. In the socialist context, state propaganda is the advertising machine that creates and channels desire.

The managerial structure of Fordism – be it capitalist or socialist – is hierarchical. Planning is always centralized to create a hierarchy of management extending from producers to consumers. For this economy to work, consumers must be convinced that they want what others want them to want. The most important product of the manufacturing process is the consumer.

It is not difficult to understand why modernist art tends toward abstraction and modern architecture favored the machine aesthetic. The abstract canvas and Bauhaus building reflect and promote the principles of Fordism. Paradoxically, while many modern artists and architects espoused utopian goals, their ideology of social transformation resembles the very socio-economic structures they claimed to be resisting.

The introduction of computers in the manufacturing process brings subtle changes whose implications are not immediately evident. These transformations far exceed the use of computers to replace intellectual effort and physical labor. Information systems alter social structures by changing the relation between production and consumption. With the emergence of sophisticated analyses of consumption made possible by advanced electronic technology, the manufacturing process becomes considerably more flexible and diversified. Instead of the manufacturer simply imposing standardized patterns of consumption on seemingly passive consumers, consumers play a more active role in determining what is produced. In other words, there is a two-way relation between supplier and consumer. In this altered economy, the consumer produces the producer as much as the producer produces the consumer. To respond to changing patterns of consumption quickly and effectively, a less centralized manufacturing structure is necessary. As power becomes decentralized, hierarchical relations give way to lateral associations until standardization and homogenization are replaced by diversification and pluralization. Products proliferate to meet ever-changing patterns of consumption. Instead of keeping up with the Joneses, it now becomes necessary to be **different** from the Joneses. In this cultural situation, the only thing that seems to unite people is the desire to be different. When heterogeneity displaces homogeneity, postmodernism is born.

Structuralism is cultural Fordism in which the master code regulates all exchanges.    Post-structuralism is cultural post-Fordism in which there is no master code to regulate exchanges.

Since gold functions in the economic system in a manner analogous to the way God functions in the religious system, the end of the go[l]d standard is the economic equivalent of the death of God. Without secure backing, value becomes relative, constantly changing and shifting. Instead of an independent reality of intrinsic worth, the "real"

**God   dies   and   is   reborn   as   money.**

God, the sacred bull, the thing itself, gold – is a signifier, image, figure. Insofar as the real is figural the figural is, in some sense, real.    In the absence of standards that are as good as gold, how can appearances be redeemed?

In 1973 fixed exchange rates gave way to floating rates of exchange. When this occurred, it became undeniable that money is not the sign of a stable "transcendental signified" but is nothing but a sign of a sign. No longer bound to a secure referent, currency is a floating signifier whose value is relative to other floating signifiers. In this groundless economy, currency is the free flow of unanchored signs.

**As**

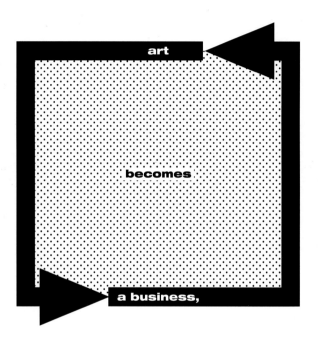

art

becomes

a business,

business becomes an art.

These two developments are inseparably

interrelated. The commodification of the

work of art reflects and extends the

aestheticization of the commodity.

**November 9, 1992**

**Dear Esa,**

Sorry I
missed your
call last
night.  I was
attending a
lecture on

that turned out to be indirectly related to our
enterprise.  Pop art represents a significant shift in
the patterns of cultural development we are
considering.  Warhol was one of the first to realize
the artistic and social significance of the media.
Pop art prefigures media philosophy.
   Our session yesterday was electric.  I am not sure
just how it differed from previous meetings.  It is
remarkable how quickly everyone is adapting to the
technology; conversation is now flowing much more
freely.  Furthermore, we are getting to know each
other so that we have a context in which to place
remarks.  While this often happens in classes, it is
strange when it occurs across an ocean.

The atmosphere of the classroom was further charged yesterday by the presence of the media. The New York Times article is quickly making an impact. By 10:00 this morning the BBC had already picked up the article and was on the phone wondering if it would be possible to come to the States to tape one of our sessions. I don't know if you noticed, but there were three photographers and two reporters in the room. The students remained marvelously oblivious to it all.

As for the substance of our exchanges, I found myself starting off in agreement with you but at one point departing from you in significant ways. I completely agree that the question we must ask continually is: How can we intervene in the realm of the imaginary? One way to approach this problem is to reread Lacan's account of the imaginary and the mirror stage in terms of telecommunications technology. The mirror in which we see ourselves reflected is not simply the eyes of the mother or those immediately around us. To the contrary, in the mediatrix, the mirror into which we gaze and that gazes at us without returning our glance is infinitely expanded. If Lacan is right, and I think he is (even if it was Hegel who initially saw this point in all of its force), when he argues that the "armor" of identity is constituted in the imaginary, then intervention in the imaginary creates the possibility of transforming subjectivity. This transformation of the subject is not limited to individual selves but must also be understood in terms of encompassing socio-cultural identities.

These insights suggest that while Marx's claim that socio-politico-cultural transformation requires assuming control of the means of production might be correct for industrial society, in post-industrial society, transformation must come about through intervention in the reproductive processes of the imaginary. I do not think that it is possible simply to take over the processes of reproduction, for the politico-economic web that is their enabling condition is far too complex for any such direct action. It is, however, possible to **intervene** in the system of the imaginary in such a way that one can use structures with and against themselves to create possibilities that were previously unavailable or repressed. This is precisely what we are attempting to do in our seminar.

As for the point on which I disagree with you: at one juncture yesterday your uneasiness with philosophy and academic discourse led you to insist that what we need is not more sophisticated analyses but the courage to be simple - the courage to cultivate a pre-philosophical state in which naive discourse on life becomes possible. I do not think discourse is ever simple. Moreover, while not everyone is philosophical in the strict sense of the term, I would insist that the kind of pre-philosophical innocence you propose is never available. The imaginary order exists before and after our own individual lives; we are born into it and shaped by it even before our personal lives begin. Consequently, there is no pre-philosophical naiveté to which we can return. Put differently, there is no way out of the imaginary web in which we are caught. This is precisely the reason we must intervene in the mediatrix to effect transformations. Our intervention, of course, is never from the outside but is always from another subject position that allows for specific disruptions. I don't think you actually believe in the pre-philosophical disposition for which you sometimes long. To get over your posture of naiveté, which I realize you do not want to get over, you must rethink your disposition as an impossible dis-position.

By the latter half of the twentieth century, the aestheticization of the commodity realized Marx's worst fears. Not only had currency become unredeemable, but money had become immaterial. With the emergence of plastic charge cards in the late 1950s and early 1960s and the introduction of computers into financial networks,

How can one locate (the) capital in cyberspace?

money became electronic. Currency, in other words, evolved from electrum (i.e. "the material substance of the ingots of which coins were made") to electricity. Electronic money is image, the play of fleeting figures on a video screen. The current that runs this economy is the fluctuating flow of electricity. Electricity is a trace of the spark that the first philosopher of flux identified with the essence of things. "All things," Heraclitus maintains, "are an equal exchange for fire, and fire for all things, as goods are for gold, and gold for goods."

Transience and ephemerality are not simply aesthetic or philosophical preferences but are economic necessities. Capitalism requires constantly expanding markets. As limits of growth are increasingly encountered, it becomes necessary to create a disposable culture in which the new is constantly desired. Changing

When money disappears in the net, its reproductive process runs wild.

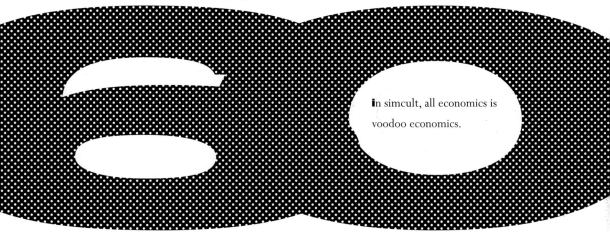

in simcult, all economics is voodoo economics.

fashions and styles becomes a way of sustaining viable markets when economic expansion comes to an end. The fashionable must be fashionable because the durable is unendurable.

**E l e c t r o n o m i c s** [9]

The **species** of the syllogism is money, and coined money is "specie." "Specie," in turn, can also designate "either of the consecrated elements of the Eucharist." Within the machinations of the mediatrix, the process of transubstantiation extends from bread and body, as well as wine and blood, to paper, gold and even electricity.

I have trouble distinguishing my bank card from my charge card.

As the mediating third that secures the unity of differences, money is the "metamorphosed shape of all commodities." Through a magic approaching alchemy, different things are, in effect, transformed into gold, which establishes "the equation of the heterogeneous." But gold is no longer gold, for it has become light. Try to put light under your mattress.

An index of the unreality of money is the disrelation between the stock market and the economy. For the past several years, the American economy has been in recession and yet the stock market continues to climb to record heights. It is as if the world of finance were an imaginary realm that had little to do with so-called actual economic conditions. Not even the crash of '87 seems to have had much impact, for the market now is much higher than it was before it fell. The only conclusion would seem to be that the economy has become hyperreal.

The market has become a supermarket of images where no one can avoid the tabloids.

When the Big Board went electric, everything became lite.

Debt is unreal if we do not have to pay it back today.

Postmodern art makes the disappearance of money appear.

When trading at a distance, space becomes insignificant; only the moment matters.

if human blood can be contaminated, what is to prevent the blood of the global economy from contracting a deadly virus?

One of the wonders of the electronic age: robbing a bank without leaving home.

Where is my safe deposit box in cyberspace?

International capital is realizing what previous revolutions have failed to accomplish: the abolition of nation states. States, of course, continue to exist; indeed, resurgent nationalism is tearing the world apart. But virulent nationalism sounds the death knell for nation states. Nations have become specters of stateless flows and currencies that slowly erode the ground on which the state is built until collapse becomes inevitable.

In simcult, every bank is an "image bank."

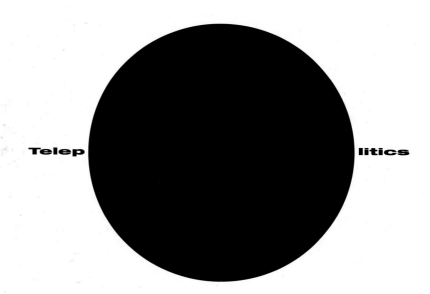Telep litics

**W**e desperately need a political economy of the image.

**M**odernity

ended on August 6, 1945.

The postmodern condition we are

living is not simply the result of having

been raised on television. As the children

of Hiroshima, we have always known

that modernity is a nightmare

from which we **must**

awake.

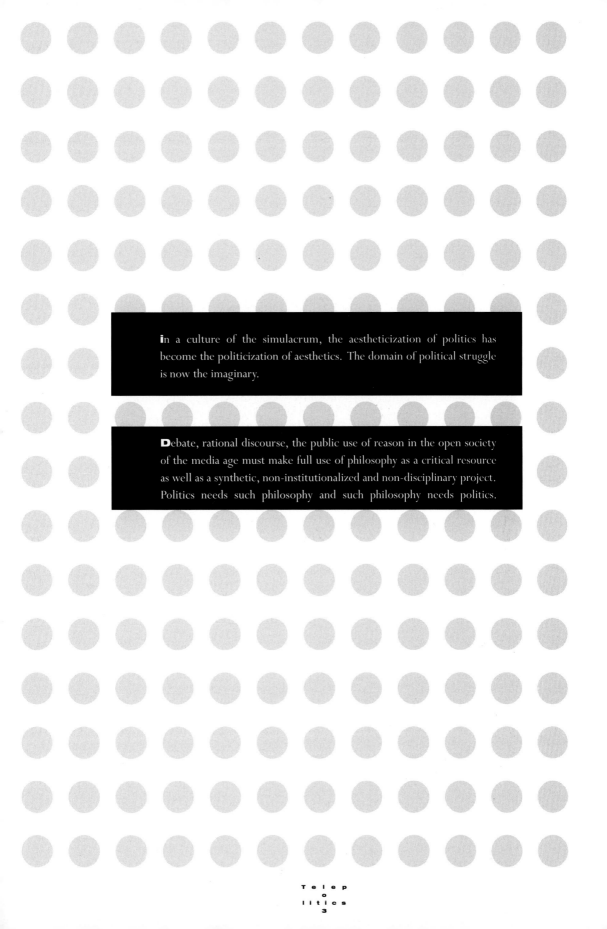

In a culture of the simulacrum, the aestheticization of politics has become the politicization of aesthetics. The domain of political struggle is now the imaginary.

Debate, rational discourse, the public use of reason in the open society of the media age must make full use of philosophy as a critical resource as well as a synthetic, non-institutionalized and non-disciplinary project. Politics needs such philosophy and such philosophy needs politics.

**November 9, 1992**

**Dear Mark,**

  A few moments before I rush to
the airport to pick up Pipsa.
  For me she's the ultimate
philosopher.  Most of the truly
important things I have learned
from her.

I speak of the naive discourse of life
because I think it is fundamental that,
in the midst of all these machines,
technologies and instrumental
powerhouses, we maintain uncommon
commonsense about values and emotions.  I
accept your criticism of my careless ways
of speaking of things like emotions and
values but do not take it seriously.
That criticism applies only to the
intellectual realm, which ultimately
doesn't count.  The notion of love may be
"deeply problematic" but the point of
love is love itself and not the notion of
love.  In the realm of life, to put it
that way, naiveté is crucial.
   Media philosophy is based on naiveté
because it is based on convictions and
desire for change.  It challenges
existing patterns of academic reasoning,
especially its commitment to conceptual

> The imaginary is a template that is open to modulation and
> modification. In simcult, the question of transformation shifts from the
> register of production to the register of reproduction. The one who
> deploys the means of reproduction controls psycho-social processes.

clarity, just as life itself does.
Paradoxically, the media generate a
certain immediacy that is inseparable
from subjective experience.  For this
reason, my respect and love for Pipsa are
directly related to my interventions in
Finnish society through the media and
public lectures, and in none of this is
conceptual clarity particularly
important.
   I am sick and tired of arguments; I am
sick and tired of the cult of expert
knowledge.  I refuse to step into the
trap set by the intelligence of our times
that says: "Anything you say can be used
against you - so better be careful in
your wordings."  I don't want to be
conceptually cautious and argumentatively
careful - that's simply not on the top of
my agenda.  I have better and, I think,
more significant, things to do.  For me
media philosophy, as a form of life in
the media age, injects an element of
sanity and hope in the midst of
all-encompassing mechanisms of conceptual
clarity and institutions of triviledge.

Simcult erases the line separating superstructure from infrastructure. Since the economy has become electronic, imaginary conflicts determine economic policies as much as economic practices determine symbolic structures.

Representation is not only a political issue: it is also an aesthetic problem:

X repr

Teledemocracy is a disguised reinvention of dictatorship. In dictatorship, only one speaks; in teledemocracy, many speak. In the first, many are lost in one; in the second, one is lost in many. Dictatorship and teledemocracy mark the end of

# esentative

government. In the former, the people become an extension of the will of the leader; in the latter, the "leader" becomes the recording surface for the will of the people.

imaginary action is not unreal. To the contrary, in simcult, real action is necessarily imaginary.

Last night one of the television networks ran a show about a young, handsome presidential candidate whose bid for the White House was threatened by a youthful fling with a beautiful woman. In the present climate, all such films have become disappointing because the "real life" soap opera of the presidential campaign is wilder than any movie could ever be. It is no longer clear whether movies rewrite the news or the news restages movies.

# In simcult, all politics is cultural politics.

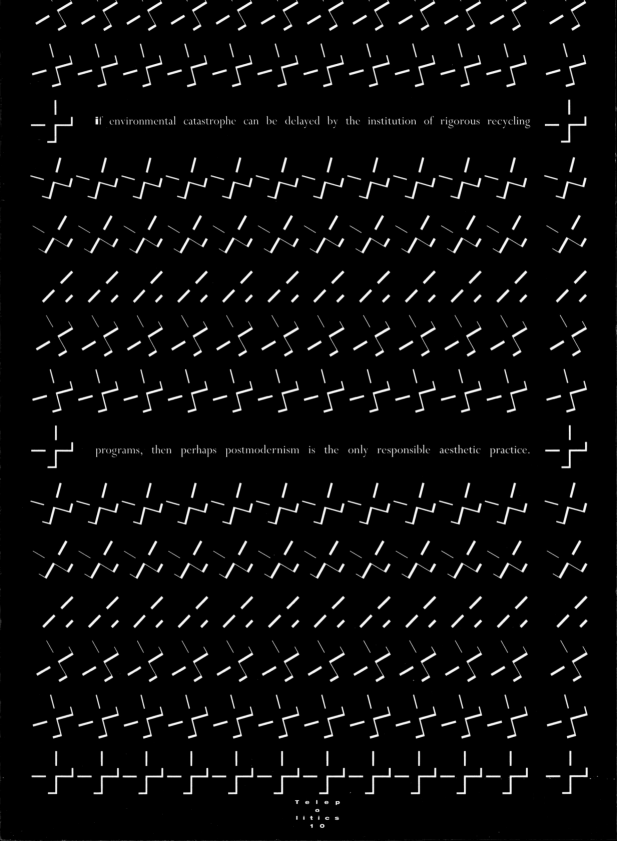

If environmental catastrophe can be delayed by the institution of rigorous recycling

programs, then perhaps postmodernism is the only responsible aesthetic practice.

Engagement must never overwhelm disengagement, and disengagement must never undercut engagement.

# Critical

involvement requires the cultivation of both the distance the insider can never maintain and the closeness the outsider can never enjoy.  Neither inside nor outside, the imagologist remains forever marginal.

**Speed**

in cyberspace speed transforms the meaning of the human race.

**M**arinetti's future has become our present. In an early manifesto, he writes: "We affirm that the world's magnificence has been enriched by a new beauty; the beauty of speed. A racing car whose hood is adorned by great pipes, like serpents of explosive breath – a roaring car that seems to run on shrapnel – is more beautiful than the Victory of Samothrace."

What, then, of machines that run at the speed of light? When the net is fiber optic, the speed of communication collapses space in a moment that is virtually instantaneous. Omnipresence descends from the heavens and becomes actual on earth. "Time and space died yesterday. We already live in the absolute, because we have created eternal, omnipresent speed."

**W**hen I become speed, the I disappears. Is it possible that the "I" becomes a "we" through speed?

Speed yields new structures of awareness. Formed within the realm of speed, perceptions attain not only new form but also fresh style and content. Under the pressure of the moment, a communicative perception dresses itself fundamentally differently from the way it is attired when it is constituted by techniques of postponement and timely indifference. The challenge of media philosophy extends all the way to the inner chambers of apparently pure thought – epistemology itself. The so-called "basic" questions of classical epistemology, as well as the justification of knowledge and theories, the problem of other minds, and the means of grounding basic principles of induction and deduction carry no special

relevance for **media philosophy.**

Abstract questions concerning general principles of justification lose their significance in the face of claims of urgency, created by the bombardment of information unleashed in the mediatrix. To think at the speed of light – this is the impossible challenge! The way we were educated in print culture does not prepare us to communicate in that urgent instant. We must start to think, perceive, criticize and synthesize in new ways that make communication in the various media both possible and profitable.

**i**n the global compu-telecommunications network, the real is digitalized and the digital is real. Along the channels of the fiber optic network, disembodied minds travel at the speed of light. As speed increases, distance decreases. Space seems to collapse into a presence that knows no absence and time seems to be condensed in a present undisturbed by past or future. If ever achieved, such enjoyment of presence in the present would be the fulfillment of the deepest and most ancient dreams of the western religio-philosophical imagination.

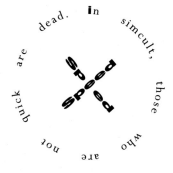

**C**yberspace is not a matter of place but of time. The no-place of cyberspace is the instant
o       f       s       p       e       e       d.

## Dear Mark,

"American philosophy"?  This truly puzzles me because I now realize,
as a result of your analysis, that with all its enormous human,
economic and creative capital, America has had so little to offer the
world in philosophy.  Brilliant technicians of argument, superb
analysts of expert problematics, gigantic intellectual achievements in
the field of technicalities.  But philosophy properly so-called,
philosophy-in-the-open or philosophy-for-the-world - America's
contribution here is strangely lacking.

One would have thought that someone would have done superbly in the
United States what I've done in Finland - broken out of the academy
into the media - radio, TV, newspapers, gossip columns - to assume a
celebrity status that makes it possible to serve as a critical
commentator on manners, morals and politics, in the languages of our
age.  In this way, the very title "philosopher" takes its place in the
public's awareness next to titles like "businessman," "artist,"
"rockstar" and "politician."  The Andy Warhol of philosophy, the
Madonna of philosophy: that's what is needed.  Media philosophy in the
USA and for the USA.

Recall that in this country I'm routinely referred to in the gossip
columns as "philosopher Esa Saarinen."  This is as the result of a
decade-long advertising campaign and product-development effort in my
personal factory of philosophy.  I'm not saying I've succeeded
spectacularly; to the contrary I've been incredibly slow to grasp
what's happening, and even slower to get my own act together.  What I
am saying is that the products you develop together with your
customers, focussing on their particular needs, are likely to differ
from products developed in a typical academic assembly line arranged by
the wisdom of the past.

Economies of scale also affect products.  For example, Journal of
Philosophy, America's most respected philosophical journal with widest
circulation, still reaches only a few thousand people.  And yet, most
academic philosophers concentrate their efforts on getting an article
published in this journal.  Let's assume very optimistically that its
potential readership is 10,000.  All the philosophy factories
throughout the USA, filled with talented experts of all brands, devoted
to product development, production and marketing for such a small
audience.  The population of Finland, a very small country in northern
Europe, is 5 million - 500 times more than that 10,000 people qualified
to read international academic philosophy in the whole world.

If it is to have any impact, "post-analytic philosophy" will have to
be more than just another collection of expert essays, another act of
analytic philosophers criticizing the presuppositions of analytic
philosophy.  Post-analytic philosophy will have to be post-academic
philosophy.  Philosophy in front of the public gaze, in short, media
philosophy.

So I am an American philosopher.  You are right.  More American than
Americans themselves because I take as my point of departure the kind
of convictions I think characterize the American spirit outside
academic philosophy: pragmatism, straightforwardness, enthusiasm in
making a genuine contribution, the conviction that one can make a
difference, and belief in the new.  And, perhaps most important,
naiveté.

**November 10, 1992**

The point is not only that politics has sped up but that speed has been politicized. Power is speed and speed is power. In the culture of the simulacrum, the swift shall inherit the earth.

if politics is the art of negotiation,

is the death of the political. Negotiation takes time and time is precisely what we don't have. The intelligent machines of today's techno-military complex reduce the time separating action and reaction to seconds or split seconds. In the instant, negotiation and deliberate decision become impossible.

Speed privileges certainty and assertion. When there is never enough time, it is necessary to make your point quickly and concisely. It is not possible to slow down long enough to allow time for uncertainty and questions. But when there is not enough time for uncertainty, certainty becomes destructive — of others and eventually of ourselves.

Telecommunications technology speeds everything up to save time. But what are we saving time for? In which bank is it stored? Does it bear any interest? How can it be withdrawn?

**November 10, 1992**

# speed

**Why** do we always slow down and speed up rather than slow up and speed down? Perhaps because we believe that speed is transcendent. But isn't it possible that transcendence is infinitely slow

**Dear Esa,**

Sorry for the confusion about the meeting time for our next class. We have to get international time synchronized! The mix-up a couple of weeks ago was the result of your change from summer time. We do not set our clocks back until this weekend. Thus, though we started with a 7 hour time difference, for the past three sessions we have had only a 6 hour time difference. Next week you want to meet one hour later than usual. But since we set our clocks back, we will not change our meeting time. In other words, one hour later for you is the same time for us. Got it? See you at 1:00, which is no longer 7:00, but is once again 8:00.

?

in a world of speed,

For the past several decades, philosophers and critics have been arguing about the end of history and the closure of the book. But these debates consistently miss the crucial point. The issue is neither philosophical nor literary but technological. History ends and the book disappears when narrative continuity collapses in the instant. Speed is the agent of this collapse. To attempt to resurrect history or reopen the book is to try to put the brakes on the speed that has become our milieu.

An axiom of the hypertextual environment: the speed of information processing is inversely proportional to the rate of retention of the information processed.

If all reading has become speed reading, then all "books" must be text-bytes. What does it mean to sink your teeth into a byte?

Speed, speed and more speed. Would it be possible for a revolution to occur so quickly that no one even noticed it?

What is the **other** of speed? What does speed leave behind?

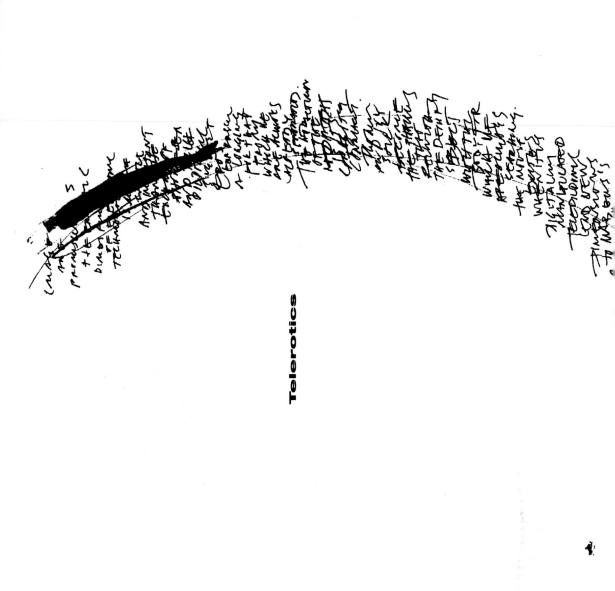

**Telerotics**

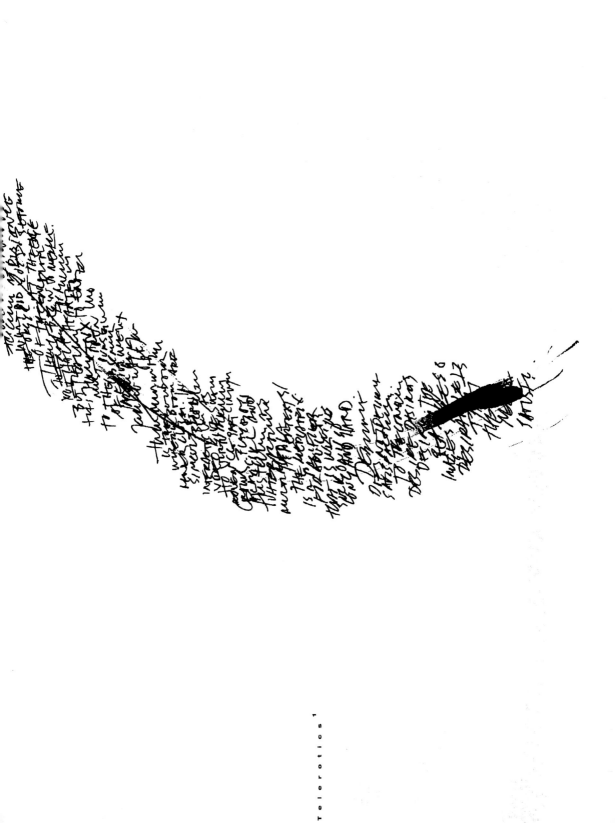

us.

cuo

mis

pro

are

ges

ima

Telerotics 2

The erotic dimension of electronic technology is more subtle and important than the excesses of phone sex and teledildonics suggest. Eros expresses a longing for that from which we are always already separated. The attraction of the mediatrix is its capacity to connect. Phone and joy stick become the phallus that reunites the desiring subject with the body for which we are always searching.

telerotics⁴ The mouse excites when it is digitally manipulated.

**T**eledildonics lend new dimensions to Ma Bell's slogan:

"Reach

out

and

touch

someone."

The ecstasy of communication is fucking at a distance.

**W**hat did you do **before** the orgy?

**At** the edge of the envelope, things begin to merge.

**To** enter the mediatrix

— not half-heartedly but really to enter the mediatrix —

we must open ourselves to the obscene surplus of enjoyment.

Jack in . . . Jack out . . . Jack off!

The mediatrix is the boudoir where doors are never closed.

In simcult porno becomes interactive. As video gives way to virtual reality, audience participation grows.

**Playboy, Playgirl** and **Hustler**

as

interactive,
multimedia
hypertexts!

The mediatrix is a pacifier for adults. That is why we suck on it so long and hard.

**D**esire does not desire satisfaction. To the contrary, desire desires desire.

The reason images are so desirable is that they never satisfy.

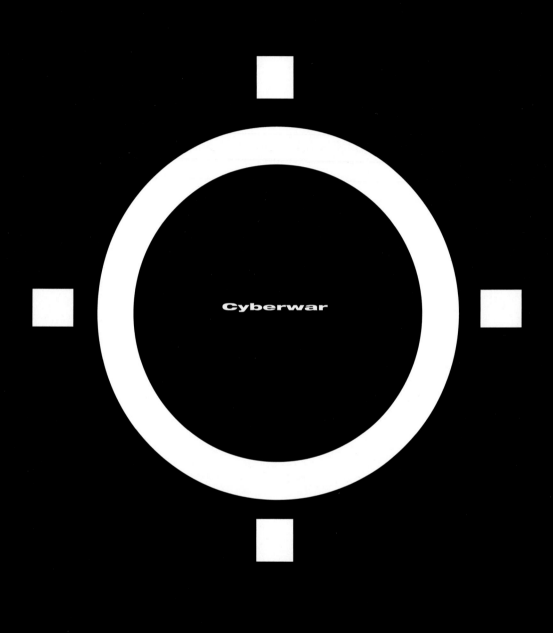

Cyberwar

In the culture of the simulacrum, every war is a war game. Both the event and pseudo-event are staged on the video screen.

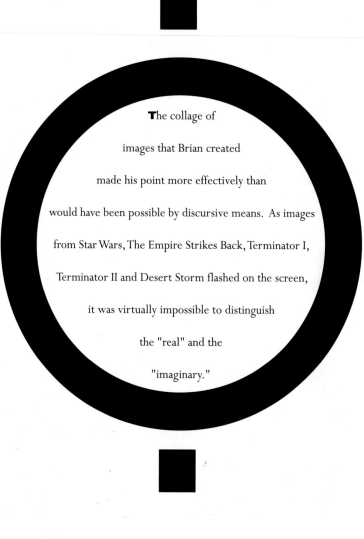

The collage of

images that Brian created

made his point more effectively than

would have been possible by discursive means. As images

from Star Wars, The Empire Strikes Back, Terminator I,

Terminator II and Desert Storm flashed on the screen,

it was virtually impossible to distinguish

the "real" and the

"imaginary."

## Dear Esa,

The play of mirrors
reached dizzying
proportions during today's
seminar.  While we were
watching Brian's video on
our screens, we were also
watching you watch the
video.  The cameras in
Helsinki were positioned
in such a way that we
could see both the video
on the monitor and you
observing the screen.  As
the images proliferated,
the play of simulacra
became completely
labyrinthine.  Utterly
baffled, I could not
decide which screen to
watch.  Perhaps more
extraordinary than the
confusion created by my
entanglement in this
endless web of the
imaginary was the uncanny
experience of watching a
video **simultaneously** in
Williamstown and Helsinki.
In cyberspace, it is
possible to be in two
places at the same time.
Where, then, are we now?

## November 11, 1992

So-called

"collateral damage"

testifies

to

the

stupidity

of

"smart"

weapons.

The battleground of the twenty-first century will be the economy. The arrival of global finance means that the economic wars of the future will inevitably be cyberwars. Where are the generals for these wars being trained?

**Cyberwar dehumanizes the most inhuman human activity.**

Since total nuclear war never takes place and hence is unreal, the reality of nuclear war is its unreality. We can "experience" nuclear war only through its deferral. The doctrine of deterrence transforms war into a simulacrum by imagining a conflict that can never take place.

i          n
cyberwar,
d  e  a  t  h
b e c o m e s
u n r e a l .

**T**hough cyberwar seems to be nothing more than a war of images, smart bombs destroy with unprecedented efficiency.

How can we forget the bomb?  How can we unlearn

what we have learned?  How can we unmake what we

have made?  And yet, if we cannot forget, unlearn and

unmake, how can we survive?

irt

uali

ty

**Signified:**

You have always offended me.

**Signifier:**

Why do you find me offensive?

**Signified:**

I don't know.  I just do not feel I really need you.

**Signifier:**

Not need me?

**Signified:**

Yeah.  I don't need you.  I know what I am.  And then you come along and screw everything up

by trying to tell everybody what you think I am. You just never get it right.

**Signifier:**

I guess I never realized you felt that way.  I surely don't want to offend you so I'll just keep quiet.

From now on, you can speak for yourself.

**T**he reality engine generates virtual worlds even when we think they are real. Who can be sure whether or not she is wearing goggles of a hidden simulator? Cultural programs, after all, code perception and cognition every bit as much as computer programs.

# Gesamtk

in

cyberspace

matter

no

longer

matters.

What,

then,

do

forms

domesticate

?

Virtual reality creates a phantasmagoria whose precursors are not only radio, television and video but extend as far back as nineteenth-century magic lanterns, panoramas and dioramas. When wearing goggles and wrapped in a body glove, the world becomes a

# unstwerk

in which the distinction between reality and illusion dissolves.

Is the mediatrix an electronic prosthesis of our organism, or are our minds and bodies psycho-physical prostheses of the immaterial web in which we are entangled?

In one of its guises, the university of the twenty-first century will be a cyberversity. As is so often the case, the shape of the future can be glimpsed in the games of youth. At this very moment, thousands of young people from all over the world are jacked into Multiple User Simulated Environments (MUSEs). Though the characteristics of these cyberspace environments vary, they usually involve participation in the elaboration of a narrative whose outline is continually changing. By accessing a MUSE, individuals are able to assume one or more characters through whom they enter cyberspace. Everything from rooms to roles can be created and changed repeatedly. What makes MUSEs so intriguing is that the story unfolds in "real" time. In other words, exchange is instantaneous and conversation is "live." Through rudimentary coding procedures, groups are formed and relations develop. It is not difficult to imagine appropriating MUSEs for educational purposes. Instead of a group narrative, it would be possible to conduct a global seminar on the net. A group of students from all over the world could meet regularly to discuss matters of common interest. The class could be as large or as small as appropriate, and meetings could be as frequent or infrequent as necessary. The lines of the cyberversity are there for those who know how to read them.

What is surprising is not that the real has become questionable but that it went unquestioned for...

ality

**November 18, 1992**

**Dear Esa,**

   Today marked another extraordinary moment in our seminar. As Cynthia projected the tape of her presentation on your screens, we simultaneously observed her image and heard her voice on our screen, saw her "real" body and heard her silence and laughter as she watched her performance, and watched you watching the tape thinking it was Cynthia talking in real time. We could not, of course, be sure whether the feed was smooth enough to leave no trace of the substitution Cynthia staged. But as time passed, it seemed as if you actually thought that Cynthia was speaking to you "in person."

   During the past several weeks, the students have become much more imaginative about the possibilities created by the media we are using. In Dana and Joel's play, Brian's cyberwar video, and Cynthia's virtual performance, we see multimedia becoming meta-multimedia. In other words, the students are beginning to see the possibility of using multimedia to analyze and criticize multimedia.

... so long.

Virtual reality is, in many ways, the inevitable conclusion of the society of spectacle. With the inexorable expansion of the mediascape, all reality is mediaized and thus becomes virtual.

In

cyberspace,

effing

the

real

is

no

longer

unthinkable.

**the Gra**

Computer-enhanced imaging transforms the apparently passive recording surface into an open space for creative design. As electronically manipulated images displace filmic images, it is impossible to be certain whether the photograph has been doctored. The changing faces of photography and video expose the fabrication of reference and the fiction of truth.

Virtual reality

**S**everal years ago, our family was driving across
the vast expanse of the West. When we
told Kirsten that it was "only" a few
more hours until we reached

# d Canyon,

she rebelled: "I don't
want to go there!
I've already seen
pictures
of it."

How will compu-telecommunications transform the museum? What happens to the archive when it is computerized? How does one display images in cyberspace? If telewriting is recasting print into something that is neither traditional speech nor writing, electronic technology harbors changes in the shape of museums that virtually no one has yet realized. The museum of the twenty-first century will, like all other institutions, be international, for, when the whole world is wired, the local is not merely local. The objects on display will undergo radical change. In the culture of the simulacrum, it will no longer be necessary to exchange the "real thing." Reproductions will become "better" than the actual object – be that object an archaeological artifact, a piece of sculpture, or a painting. It is possible to imagine a museum constructed in cyberspace where objects from the entire world are assembled for display. Furthermore, just as telewriting allows readers to become writers, so the museum of the future will allow viewers to become curators. Imagine a museum with an inexhaustible image file and multiple paths that allow navigation through the archive. Each person could, then, assemble an exhibition from whatever point of view seemed interesting or for whatever occasion seemed relevant. For more than a century, the model of the museum has been the encyclopedia. Having realized the futility of the enlightenment project of the encyclopedia, the museum of the future will be hypertextual.

The name of the new museum will be: The Cybermuseum. There will be great resistance to this new institution. Critics will bemoan the disappearance of the art object and insist that the reproduction cannot do justice to the "real" thing. In launching this critique, all of the resources of the metaphysics of presence will be invoked to reinvest the original work of art with its unique aura. But the struggle to save the encyclopedic museum is futile because its time has passed.

The cumbersome goggles of today's virtual reality machines are merely transitional objects to more compact and efficient devices. The day will come when goggles will take the form of eyeglasses or even contact lenses. Then the televisual era will look like the primitive past.

Virtual

# "the omn
# of

Why do some simulacra become part of the "real" world? If everything is image, why do certain images not appear to be images? Is the constitution of the real a product of fandom?

reality is the technological realization of Freud's

# potence
# thought. "

In virtual worlds, thought becomes reality and reality becomes imaginary. With the flick of my head, I remold the world and transform what I see, hear and feel.

# Virtuality

is    irreality.

The police officer thought the toy gun was real and shot the youth "in self-defense." Don't try to tell the parents of the dead child that the fake gun was unreal. The cold corpse testifies to the deadly reality of the simulacrum.

**November 20, 1992**

## Dear Mark,

Imagologies, as a critical and cultural investigation into the functioning and forms of production of the image technologies of our time, sets itself within the tradition that Foucault describes as a critical inquiry into ourselves. Like Kant's essays on the Enlightenment and the French Revolution, as well as Foucault's archaeology, imagologies aims at "problematizing its own discursive present-ness: a present-ness which it interrogates as an event, an event whose meaning, value and philosophical singularity it is required to state, and in which it is to elicit at once its own **raison d'étre** and the foundation of what it has to say."

It seems hard to avoid the conclusion that if we take Foucault's problematics of our own present-ness seriously, then something like a critico-cultural analysis of simulacra, images, and virtual realities of the postmodern - an analysis of the flat, electric, digital net of the present - is an utmost necessity. Imagologies represents Foucault's analysis of the present in the present, the present that is ours - the present of the age of media.

By linking imagologies to Foucault's project and the critical inquiry into an ontology of ourselves, we can understand in a fresh light two aspects of imagologies that a more conventional student probably will find maddening about the enterprise undertaken in this "book." First, the conventional philosopher is likely to feel unattracted by the insistent emphasis imagologies place on contingent technicalities and context-bound production mechanisms of simulacra. How can philosophy address itself so outrightly to contingent matters of engineered, technicized origin? The answer is that this is how the ontology of ourselves must be written in an engineered, technological age. Since we are contingently technicized, so must be the description of our present-ness. Second, the conventional philosopher is likely to feel uneasy about the apparently descriptive aspects of the project of imagologies. As self-respecting philosophers, should we not address ourselves to "the general problem of representation," instead of the minutiae of the functioning of a particular system of representation (i.e. email, women's magazines, talk shows, teleseminars, etc.)? But the point is that nominalism and descriptivism are as necessary in imagologies as they are in Foucault's work on hospitals, prisons and other historical micropowers. Imagologies is an effort to analyze key micropowers of our present-ness - the micropowers of contingent media institutions.

The gravity of such a project gains momentum by the fact that in a technicized, praxis-driven and accelerated world, any description of the present is always already a has-been. The techniques of the postmodern always involve more than any description of them can yield. Description inevitably falls behind, and more and more so, as progress becomes exponential. Thus, imagologies aims at self-understanding and self-determination in an age during which self-understanding and self-determination have become technically close to impossible.

Media form us, and each of us is a media figure. Each of us is a simulacrum, even the traditional, conventional academic philosopher, who, in his effort to join the eternal, is the simulacrum of his hopeless, historic, technically impossible ideal.

In a twist of realism, an imagologist does not place herself outside the domain of analysis. Her experience of the present is an integral part of the object of study. The imagologist is concerned to determine - in the words of Foucault - how she, "as a philosopher, forms a part of this same process [being analyzed], and . . . how [she] has a certain role to play in this process, figuring in it, that is to say, at once as an element and as an actor."

The addition "as an actor" is particularly explosive. It points to a task and a battlefield that philosophy - intellectualism at large - has done its best to avoid. Not only do we face, in imagologies, our present-ness in the media and through the media as an object of study and a field of intellectual analysis, we also face a play into which we have been thrown, the play of our present, the play that is presently played everywhere around us. It is a play in which we must act even though we lack a manuscript, an understanding of our role, and a guarantee of the ultimate fall of the curtain.

And act she does, the fool, that inspired amateur-in-media-inscribing, the actor of imagologies:

the media philosopher.

in the culture of the simulacrum, how does one **face** reality?

The point is not simply that truth and reality have been absorbed by illusion and appearance. Something far more subtle and unsettling is taking place. Somewhere Nietzsche suggests that when reality is effaced, appearances disappear as well. What emerges in the wake of the death of oppositions like truth/illusion and reality/appearance is something that is neither truth nor illusion, reality nor appearance but something else, something other. This other is as yet unnamed.

**N**othing is real.

The real is nothing.

**R** e - p r e s e n t a t i o n     i s

**B o d y**

_atelier'_

Body Snatching

de-presentation.

natching [1]

**Body Snatching**

For several months, he had insisted that he wanted to live until his 80th birthday, but did not care if he survived longer. Fulfilling his desire was far from easy, for, in the months prior to his birthday, he suffered several heart attacks. On one occasion, he had to be revived four times by electric shock. The family reluctantly decided not to administer shock treatment again. But a fifth shock was unnecessary; he slowly recovered and was able to travel north to celebrate his birthday.

The party held in his honor was hardly festive. Since everyone knew this would be his last birthday, a melancholy cloud hung over the event. As if to confirm these suspicions, his grandson was intent on recording the event on video tape. He interviewed his grandfather and all the guests. The presence of the video camera transformed the entire atmosphere of the gathering by making the birthday party seem unreal. The occasion was less a celebration than an event staged in order to be recorded. It was as if everyone interviewed were saying: "We know you are not dead quite yet, but we want to get this on tape so that we can remember you when you are gone." The camera, in effect, created the event by stealing the body.

Again, the old man's wish was granted. In less than three months, he was dead. I have not yet looked at the video and I doubt I ever will.

Our task:
to think the elision
of the world.

## Everything is simulacrum.

The question is whether this claim represents an ontological or an epistemological shift. In other words, has there been a fundamental change in our world that makes it substantially different from previous epochs, or have we finally realized what has always been the case? Has the real died and been reborn in the imaginary register, or has the so-called real always been a simulacrum that has not been recognized as such?

From one point of view, it seems that, in spite of radical technological developments, there has been no substantial change that makes our world qualitatively different from previous worlds. Accordingly, an ontological shift does not seem to have taken place and the changes we have undergone appear to be epistemological. If this is so, we would have to claim something like a universal truth: every notion of truth, reality, etc., has always been mistaken, for the true and the real are always already simulacra. But the culture of the simulacrum makes it impossible to establish universal claims of any kind. Epistemological or ontological? The question remains undecidable.

**C**ompu-telecommunications deterritorializes every thing and every body.

The perversions of philosophy run deep beneath your skin.

**i**mage exposes one to the gaze of others, which simultaneously captivates and liberates. The captivated image becomes captivating when it liberates associative energies that generate new images.

**i**f the texts of grand narratives were still believable, one might imagine a philosopher arguing that the history of the twentieth century is the story of the progressive dematerialization of culture. As life increasingly imitates art, abstraction and formalism begin to characterize all aspects of experience until the world begins to pale.

Live broadcast of sporting events and political rallies. Simulcast concerts. Electronic presidency. Films and videos of performances. Tapes of touring bands. Classes held on video screens in "real" time. Does it any longer make sense to speak of live performances when everything becomes an instant replay?

In the mediatrix, no event is a pseudo-event because every event is a pseudo-event.

**The jargon of authenticity no longer rings true on the telephone.**

**Dear Esa,**

On Wednesday, someone from
National Public Radio is coming to
do a program on the seminar.  We
will save time at the end of the
session for her to interview you
and your students.

**November 21, 1992**

**No** thing              matters.

No **thing**              matters.

Nothing     **matters.**

But what does it mean to matter when all appears to be a simulacrum?

## Dear Esa,

When I returned home after our first seminar, there was a package waiting for me in the mail. It was from a woman I do not know who had attended the memorial service we had held for my father the previous week. She had sent me a kind note with a video of a television program that had featured my father's efforts to create a natural park in the suburban town where he lived. After he retired, my father devoted much of his time and energy to establishing this natural preserve and developing an environmental studies curriculum for teachers and students from elementary school through high school. A teacher all his life, he worked with young people in the park until the day he died.

For several months, I have not been able to view the video. Finally, last night when no one else was home, I watched the tape. It was an excruciatingly difficult experience that was much more distressing than looking at photographs or movies. Video mixes audio and visual effects in a way that is uniquely real. The tone of voice, the subtlety of gesture, the turns of phrase. It is all so lifelike. The simulacrum is not only the trace of the disappearance of the real; the image itself becomes reality. For a few disorienting moments, Dad was present again. The very vitality of the simulacrum made the "reality" of the cold corpse to which I bid farewell two months ago all the more overwhelming.

As I watched the tape of the television program, I suddenly realized that my father recognized the stakes of media philosophy before we did. Indeed, he was practicing it before we conceived it. The TV program and countless newspaper and magazine articles proved to be very powerful in advancing the cause to which he devoted the last years of his life. Not bad for a man in his eighties.

Something very interesting is beginning to happen in the students' email conversation. The women in the class are much more uneasy about the "out-of-body" experience they are having than the men. Cynthia and Kaisu are obsessed with email and yet are deeply disturbed by the evaporation of the material and the absence of the face-to-face. The men in the class are much less bothered by all of this.

The culture of the simulacrum is, paradoxically, both an "anoxeric culture" and a "culture of the body." As the real disappears into the hyperreal, the body becomes an obsessive preoccupation. Never has the concern with body image been greater. Concentration on the body can lead either to its excessive denial or its excessive affirmation. Self-denial and self-decoration are contrasting styles of make-up. And make-up is always a make-over that transforms nature into culture.

The (dis)order of the simulacrum is a facelift for the real.

Last night I stopped reading Howard Rheingold's **Virtual Reality** long enough to go to a lecture by a leading contemporary artist, Kiki Smith, whose work concentrates on the human body. What is most striking about Smith's art is her preoccupation with body parts that are usually invisible. Mouths, anuses, stomachs, intestines, muscles and brains are exposed in all their horrible beauty. The auditorium was packed and the audience was entranced. Why is Smith's art so popular at this particular moment? Why has the body become the preoccupation of so many in our culture? Perhaps Rheingold's book holds a clue. In virtual worlds, the body disappears or is displaced by a so-called artificial prosthesis. As the materiality of experience vanishes, the need to reaffirm it grows intense.

Body Snatching

**W**here do I meet my body in the net?

Natural foods, natural fabrics, natural medicine, natural this, natural that. The concern with the natural is an index of its disappearance. In the postmodern world, nature is cultivated through the simulacrum by an advertising industry in which image is all. To buy into the natural is to reaffirm precisely what one wishes to deny: that the artificial is all we can experience or know.

To inhabit cyberspace is to be inhabited by the inhuman.

The disappearance of the referent is the appearance of (the) no-thing.

Ephemeral, fleeting, transitory. Fast lane, fast food, fast culture. In the disposable society, everything becomes detritus, rubbish, refuse. Nothing lasts.

The simulacrum is a **novum** that is neither original nor copy, real nor imaginary, signified nor signifier. The operation of the simulacrum transfigures the body.

Gazing into my terminal, watching flashes of light and bits of current dash across the screen, I am plugged into a mediatrix whose reach exceeds my grasp. Everything becomes lighter and lighter and lighter; vertigo approaches. The screen of the desert is the desert of the screen – a site of desertion, which, perhaps, has always already taken place. The screen becomes an oven in which the real is incinerated, leaving only cinders and ashes. What remains without remaining must be mourned without end.

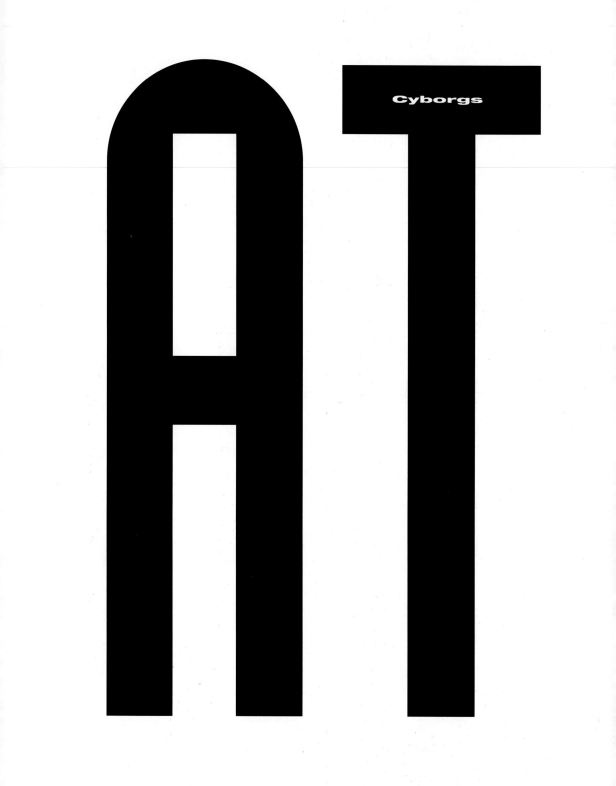

Cyborgs

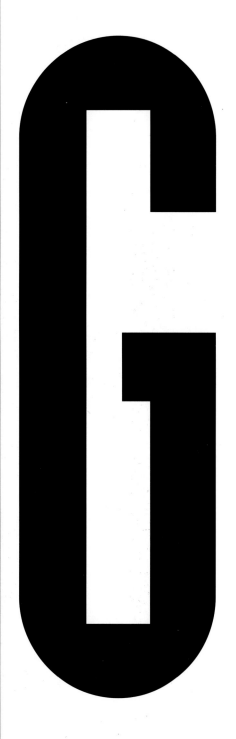

The arrival of the cyborg is made possible by the gradual removal of the barrier separating exteriority and interiority, as well as public and private space. This collapse of differences proceeds in two directions at once: from outer to inner and, conversely, from inner to outer. On the one hand, the body is progressively colonized by prosthetic devices. Implants, transplants, artificial organs, artificial insemination, genetic engineering and synthetic drugs make it harder and harder to be sure where the so-called human ends and the non-human begins. On the other hand, artificial wombs, test-tube babies, artificial intelligence and computer literacy "externalize" bodily and mental functions to such an extent that the outer is not more merely outer and the inner is not simply inner. No longer purely human, we are not yet replicants. When William Gibson and his fellow cyberpunks extrapolate from the present to the near-future, they see a world where latter-day golems pose unimaginable threats and unthinkable possibilities. If every "natural" organ can be infinitely replaced by "artificial" devices and the entire contents of the mind can be preserved by being downloaded into the matrix, the dream of immortality would seem to be realizable.

As one moves from a model of mechanical production to electronic reproduction, it is necessary to shift from the framework of dialectical materialism to non-dialectical immaterialism. The dematerialization of culture presupposes material transformations which, in turn, change the conditions of production and reproduction. Traditional oppositions like substructure/superstructure and depth/surface are not adequate for understanding these complex processes. Indeed, the very notions of materiality and immateriality, as well as the human and the inhuman, must be rethought. In the age of silicon chips and DNA programs, it is no longer possible to be certain where the material ends and the immaterial begins.

Several years ago, with a suddenness that was jolting, sugar suddenly became a poison to my system. What had been a source of energy became the cause of fatigue. Life changed in that moment in ways I still cannot calculate. From then on, the natural and the unnatural became impossibly confused for me. Without artificial chemical prostheses, I can no longer live. Indeed, nothing natural lives without the artificial. And vice versa.

No longer sugar but a **substitute** – a substitute named EQUAL. The name is richly suggestive because it is formulated to erase the very distinction it embodies. If EQUAL is equal, the artificial and the natural are indistinguishable. The message of this sugar substitute is the message of a culture of the simulacrum. Nature becomes artifice and no one can tell the difference. For many, this confusion is a disaster. For me, it is the condition of life.

This issue does not simply involve matters of sugar and sweetness. One can, after all, live without sugar. But the chemical prostheses that sustain my life do not end with sugar; I depend on another more critical substitute – **synthetic** insulin. Without the products of recombinant DNA, my so-called natural body would be dead. Three times a day I inject an "artificial" substance into my body. I suppose one could call this an addiction of sorts. The fate of being an insulin junkie is hardly an easy one. While I would never suggest that all drugs and addictions are life-sustaining, I am coming to suspect that the differences are not as great as those who have the health and wealth to be moralistic usually insist. As I slip the syringe into my leg, I realize that I share more with the addict in the ghetto than I ever dreamed possible.

For many critics, genetic research is the paradigm of technology's Frankensteinian possibilities. Apocalyptic tales and images of mutant genes run wild are fabricated to scare people into putting an end to such research. Though possible dangers should not be ignored, it would be foolish not to proceed with this area of research in a deliberate and responsible way. Without genetic engineering, I probably would already be dead. I can continue to live only because I have become a cyborg.

In the age of cyborgs, do people evolve into machines or do machines evolve into people? Where **is** the person/machine line to be drawn? Indeed, is it any longer possible to draw such a line?

**E**lectronic media are supplements to the human organism. Computers become the brains, engines the legs, video cameras the eyes, telephones the ears, and wires the nerves, veins and arteries of the world organism. The lifeblood of this corporate body is electricity. When the blood flows, the globe becomes a cyborg.

**V**irtual reality is a seeing-aid. By extending my field of vision, electronic sensors and computer displays make the invisible visible. Suddenly I can glimpse radioactivity, and electricity; I can even see inside objects and bodies that otherwise are completely opaque. With such x-ray vision, every person becomes Superman. Perhaps the reason they have stopped publishing Superman comics is that the fantasy has become real.

# December 3, 1992

**Dear Esa,**

There were moments during
yesterday's seminar when I began
to feel that postmodernism is
more American than European.
The American students were
repeatedly bothered by the
effort of the Finnish students
to appeal to a dimension of life
or experience that eludes
simulacra. When Tumi argued
that the media are not all that
important in our lives, the
students on this end sighed in
disbelief. Have the media
colonized America more
effectively than Europe? Or are
the Americans simply more aware
of their colonial status?
Yesterday I also began to feel
a generation gap more acutely
than ever before. Our students
are postmodern without even
realizing it. They live
unselfconsciously what we
theorize all too
self-consciously. Where, then,
do you and I stand in relation
to all of this? Our place is
marginal: unlike most of our
senior colleagues, as well as
many in our own generation, we
realize that a radical change is
under way and find this
situation rich with possibility;
unlike our students, this new
world is not - and probably
never will be - our own. Our
task, therefore, is twofold: to
those who are unaware or resist
change, we must bring awareness
and overcome resistance; to
those who are immersed in the
new world that is already
arriving, we must bring critical
self-consciousness and encourage
creative resistance.

**T**he dream of artificial intelligence (AI) is to replicate or replace the human mind; the dream of intelligence amplification (IA) is to extend and expand human sensation and cognition. In cyberspace, it becomes possible to integrate AI and IA to create a machinic organism that is a cyborg of cyborgs. If this super-cyborg can be interfaced with the human organism, which has itself become a cyborg, evolution might proceed by quantum leaps instead of incremental steps. Who or what will write the programs for this evolution?

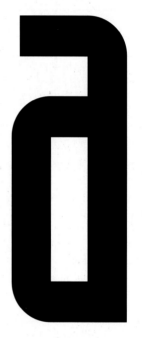

As man becomes an appendage of machines, evolution shifts from the organism to the mechanism. When the number of computers linked reaches a critical mass, some networks gain the capacity for spontaneous generation. Programs and computations unplanned by designers suddenly begin to appear.

In cyberspace, I can change my self as easily as I change

clothes.  Identity becomes infinitely plastic in a play of

## Shifting Subjects

images that knows no end.  Consistency is no longer a

virtue but becomes a vice; integration is limitation.

With everything always shifting, everyone is no one.

**A**s power is laterally dispensed throughout the mediatrix, eccentricity moves center stage.

**T**he fundamental philosophical problem in the West is the problem of the one and the many. From its beginnings in ancient Greece, western philosophy has identified being with oneness or unity and non-being with manyness or plurality. To be is to be one. But simcult changes all of this. One of the most significant marks of the advent of modernity and its extension in postmodernity is a reversal of the relative value attributed to the one and the many. In contemporary culture, oneness and unity are regarded as non-being, while manyness and plurality are believed to characterize being. The cultural imperative is no longer: "Get your shit together!" But: "Let it hit the fan!"

**I**f to desubstantialize is to deindividualize, the advent of the media age marks the disappearance of the subject.

**December 10, 1992**

**Dear Mark,**

I hope you enjoyed the transmission
of the image by Rosa Liksom with which
we began yesterday's seminar. Rosa is
one of the leading younger artists in
this country. She is also an
original, strange writer with a growing
reputation abroad. Rosa has been
following our teleseminar as a
semi-outsider and has been enjoying the
discussions tremendously. The painting
I showed last night is the first in a
series of "electric hyperworks," which,
she says, have been directly inspired
by the seminar.
Rosa is something like an imagologist
**avant la lettre.** She was an instant
success and quickly achieved cult
status in Finland. From the outset,
she has systematically refused to be
interviewed in the Finnish media and,
during the first years of her career,
there were practically no photographs
of her available. Nobody knew what she
looked like. At the opening of one
exhibition of her paintings in
Helsinki, rumor spread that Rosa Liksom
would be personally present. Hundreds
of people showed up only to find ten
eccentric-looking people present, all
dressed in similar army clothes,
introducing themselves as Rosa Liksom.

Shifting

The media people were furious. Representatives of the media, like members of the university, do not want to laugh at themselves. Excited by their emerging strength, media figures are often reluctant to concede their role as mediating interest-generating institutions for a consuming public. There is little talent for self-irony in the media. In the absence of the irony necessary for self-criticism, the media must be seduced into cooperation. The problem for so-called serious culture is that this process of seduction is likely to appear cheap.

And cheap it is, if for no other reason than the fact that the emerging product is always vulnerable to instantaneous, openly associative evaluations by irritated, disoriented others who happen to have had a bad day and refuse to listen to what you are trying to communicate. Because you are subject to cheap evaluations, you become cheap. Media philosophy is, therefore, undeniably cheap. But cheapness is not to be avoided. To the contrary, a media philosopher is a cheap trick and enjoys it.

Just yesterday I experienced a few moments of cheap excesses in a live entertainment program. I had promised to participate because the topic was supposed to be Finnish independence day. When I arrived at the studio, I discovered that I would have four and a half minutes for my interview and then perhaps eight minutes for a discussion between me, the host and one other guest. Not much time, I thought, but that's all there is.

In due course, my turn came. With the usual walking-through-a-lighted-tunnel, studio audience applauding, and music blaring, I arrived on stage. I managed to get out three or four sentences of some

Subjects[2,3] significance before the host said with excitement in his voice that there would be a surprise guest coming up, a Green activist from central Finland. As she approached the stage, she immediately fixed her attention on me and completely disregarded the host. "Now there's a man I've always wanted to kiss," she said. Catching me unaware, she grabbed me and kissed me in front of the cameras. After this, the host intervened, with laughter, explaining that "the Green activist," was, in fact, an actress, which, of course, all the TV spectators knew. The idea was to see how "an experienced TV talk show guest" would respond to a live situation that proceeded unexpectedly.

Very funny, corny, but above all, cheap. I can understand why not all professors of philosophy want to find themselves in situations like this. I must say that even I found this setting somewhat uncomfortable. Fortunately, I did wear my golden brown silk suit, matching tie, and my famous polka-dot shoes. The truth is that whatever ideas concerning the significance of the independence of the Republic of Finland I had in mind were hardly appropriate in the setting of this program. Nevertheless, I would insist that this was an excellent instance of media philosophy at its cheapest.

Even better things were to come that week. A friend called and suggested that I might be interested in a certain magazine **Erotiikan maailma** (The World of Erotics), special double issue 8/9, 1992. I was somewhat surprised because this particular publication (sold only in transparent, sealed packages) is a straightforward hard-core porno magazine that makes **Hustler** look like grandmother´s stuff. On the inside back cover, facing an explicit act scene, I found a comic strip entitled "Mälli lentää" ("Jerk flies"), with the subtitle "On the Terrace of Albert´s Street (the street I live on).

murdEr of thE REAL

Real is
LEAVING us
and escaping

Rosa -93

SPEED is VIOLANCE
and
VIOLANCE is
REAL
Rosa-93
highway Heels

Subjects 4, 5

Two women are talking: "Hey, checkit out; isn´t that Esa Saarinen, the philosopher?" "You mean the guy that wrote a fictional book about his erection on Albert´s Street?" (One collection of my essays is entitled "Erection on Albert´s Street".) "Fictional?" the other woman asks. I´m featured at this juncture with an enormous hard-on, opposite a doorman that says, "No room left for standing" ("standing" has a double meaning in Finnish). The women continue: "Fictional or not, there´s a man I´d like to come under." "Now that´s a fact." That´s media philosophy. Cheap, incredibly.

During the same week, I also participated in a 90-minute radio talk show on the status of Finnish banks, and in a travel program on Singapore. This fairly active media week will be followed next week by a 90-minute live TV-broadcast on New Age spirituality, UFOs and miraculous cures.

It seems fair to conclude that the site of communication has changed dramatically. Technologies intervene, indeed they change the flow of logic and the whole paradigm of objectified, impersonal, unemotional, distanced policies of critical, synthetic thought. I think this intervention is creative; it opens the possibility of stepping into the crowd.

The everyday, let us recall, is corny. Truth is corny, the morning shit is corny. The US presidential campaign, the best in years, that's corny. Insurance men, look-alike philosophers, so-called intellectuals, in a midtown hotel, attending their annual meeting - corny. Somebody famous fucking somebody not so famous, corny, corny, corny. A Wittgenstein joke, corny. People arguing their heads off over the analytic-synthetic distinction, people in pursuit of tenure, people placing emphasis and locating relevant literature in the expert journals, now that's truly corny.

**P**ostmodernism, Jameson argues, involves a transformation of time and the self. In the postmodern world,

historical duration in which past and future are meaningfully integrated with the present gives way to an

immersion in the present that represses the past and excludes the future. Immediacy displaces duration to

create a flux that is endless. As a result of the collapse of historical time, the self is fragmented. When

subjectivity is nothing more than a collection of momentary instants, schizophrenia becomes a generalized

cultural condition.

What Jameson describes in his characterization of postmodern experience conforms precisely to Kierkegaard's depiction of aesthetic existence. For a better account of postmodernity than Jameson is able to deliver, reread the first volume of **Either-Or.**

Decentering involves a pluralization that is neither covertly integrated nor overtly schizophrenic.

From Augustine to Hegel and Husserl, the notion of an integrated subject is bound to coherent narrative structures. Narrativity joins past and future in a present where recollection and anticipation intersect. Video shatters subjectivity by launching an assault on narrativity from two directions. On the one hand, video can speed up events until narrative sequence collapses into a high velocity flux. On the other hand, video can slow down events until they snap the line of narrative by its infinite extension. When experience is videoized, patterns of cohesion shift; line becomes montage.

Ii we rethink the disappearance of the

subject in terms of telecommunications

technology, it might be more accurate to

argue that the postmodern subject

becomes a medium. Perhaps it is less

misleading to speak of the mediaization

of the subject than of its disappearance.

For the imagologist, subjectivity is always an act of
impersonation that renders unmasking impossible.
There is more at stake in the ancient association of
"person"
with

# p    e    r    s    o    n

During the last years of his life, my father could not sleep at night. As he lay in bed waiting for the rest that would never come, he would often listen to the radio. His loneliness irrestibly drew him to late-night talk shows. As anyone who has listened to the radio when most people are sleeping knows, the later the hour, the freer the conversation. Frequently, my father would say to me: "I just can't believe what people talk about on the radio. Why would they want to expose their personal lives in that way?"

In simcult, there are no life lines.

Lacan's notion of the imaginary illuminates the way in which the order of simulacra functions. The infant, according to Lacan, is born a fragmented rather than an integrated subject. Plagued by "primal discord," the unity of the self is first apprehended in and through an other. At the mirror stage of development, which occurs between the first six and eighteen months of life, the child encounters the image of itself in the eyes of the m-other. Divided in itself, the emerging subject assumes a paranoic identity by appropriating its spectral image. Instead of unifying the subject, this act of identification further alienates the self by positing its unity **in** and **as** an other.

In contrast to the imaginary, Lacan develops an account of what he describes as the symbolic order. Drawing on Saussure's distinction between **la langue** and **la parole,** Lacan maintains that the symbolic order is the network of cultural codes, rules and laws that structure and maintain individual and social organisms. Existing both before and after the birth of the subject, the symbolic order determines the subject positions into which the individual is born. In his account of both the imaginary and symbolic orders, Lacan insists that supervening images and structures determine the identity of the subject.

It is, however, possible to push Lacan's analysis in new and different directions. Lacan correctly insists on the inextricable relation between identification and disidentification in the early stages of human development. Furthermore, images do play an essential role in the constitution of the subject. Identity is never an established fact; it is always a possibility that one approaches without ever realizing. Identity formation does not conclude with the end of infancy but continues throughout life. In order to give an adequate account of this process, it is necessary to reformulate Lacan's analysis in such a way that the interplay between the imaginary and the symbolic becomes clearer.

The imaginary that plays a determinative role in the formation of subjectivity is not limited to the maternal gaze but is constituted by the entire range of images with which the subject is bombarded throughout his or her life. Furthermore, it is not possible to separate the imaginary and symbolic orders. On the one hand, the socio-cultural reach of the imaginary extends its function to the domain that Lacan defines as symbolic. The expanded symbolic order, on the other hand, plays a critical role in determining the identity of the subject.

When understood in this way, it becomes clear that the imago-symbolic order is not unchanging but is historically constituted and thus constantly developing. Changes in the constituting order of images and symbols are, to a large extent, a function of the diverse technologies that are available in a given historical period. The technologies of subjectivity are as various as the different machines of production and reproduction that characterize different societies. If the imago-symbolic is neither universal nor unchanging, then it is possible to intervene in this order to transform the structures that condition self and society. To change the imago-symbolic order is to change the very conditions of subjectivity and sociality. From this point of view, the alienation effect wrought by identification with the imago-symbolic order becomes the presupposition for psycho-social transformation. In simcult, the imago-symbolic order is a contested domain where the personal becomes political and the political becomes personal.

The mediatrix is the imaginary register in which the subject is
constituted by the gaze of the other. As the other's other, I am a
libidinal object that is a target of uncontrollable desire. The
image triggers an immediate response that conveys a sense of
"the omnipotence of thoughts." Far from passive, the voyeur is
the private eye whose vision creates his client. The screen is a
sieve whose holes beckon Pricking Toms.

**T**he communicative intellect lives **for others.**

No longer a Cartesian subject cut off from social

and natural worlds, the one who chooses to

communicate not only enters the media but

becomes a medium whose life is a message for

others. In the mediatrix, the circle of

**W**ithin the signifying field of the culture of the simulacrum, my image is always out of control. I never know what signals I am sending or what images I am projecting. As signals and images are recorded and transmitted, the absence of mastery is magnified. The electronic dissemination of images fulfills an ancient fear of writing. When the living word "falls" into writing, the father is no longer master of his "own" son.

self-referentiality becomes an unbounded web of

relations that unravels the subject of narcissism.

Net Effect

To resist electronic technology is as futile as trying to turn
back the tides.  It has already swept over us in ways we have
yet to realize.  It is not a question of whether to accept or
reject this new world but of who is going to use it and how.
To resist the possibilities opened by the mediatrix is to leave
this  extraordinary  technology  in  the  hands  of  others.

The mediatrix grabs you, consumes you, devours you.  Its liberation becomes a bondage.

I **cannot** pull the plug.

December 1, 1992

## Dear Mark,

There are two separate TV cr
coming to cover our seminar thi
week, so please note the follow
technical matters.

1. The first TV crew will
interview us before the seminar
which means that we may have to
start the session a bit late.
will then shoot some coverage d
the seminar as we take off.

2. The other TV crew will a
during the second hour of the
seminar and, as they put up the
lights and stuff, some disrupti
might arise. I had agreed earli
that the second group would sho
even though their piece will no
aired until the spring. Since
not want to postpone their comi
the seminar, I decided to squee
them both in the same session.

With imagologies, philosophy enters the marketplace.

To philosophize in simcult is to move out of the cloister.

Might not electronic media make it possible for the first

time to develop a philosophy that is truly worldly?

Everyone has become accustomed to being on stage, so I don't expect the discussion to be effected negatively by all this.

in the rhizomic logics of the mediatrix, lines of

communication fold and refold but never unfold.

# Ex-pli

is impossible,

# com-
# -pli

is inevitable.

Simcult seems to be hopelessly anti-intellectual. But
what appears to be anti-intellectualism is actually a call
for alternative intellectual practices. The reigning

definition of the intellectual is bound to obsolete
technologies of production that bar the imagination. On
the assembly line of knowledge, the intellectual produces
print, which, in turn, produces the intellectual.
Networking unravels these cycles of production and
reproduction to create new intellectual instrumentalities.
The intellectual who remains devoted to print culture

becomes a vestigial organ that gradually withers away
without leaving a trace.

**Y**ou can never get all the bugs out.

**Postmodernism** is supposed to be characterized by the death of metanarratives that give comprehensive explanations of the world and overall direction for conduct. But those who interpret the postmodern condition in this way fall victim to one of the persistent traps of postmodern theorizing. Once again endorsing the assumption of the primacy of the textual, they assume that the battle is between conceptualized literary narratives. Since texts are what count as primary, the diagnostics of our era are carried out vis–vis textualities. Reading postmodern theoreticians, one is puzzled to observe how the earth-moving implications of the techno-structures of world production and commerce, as well as the administrative networks, go unnoticed even in the writings of the brightest and wittiest. The reason that the theoreticians of the postmodern remain imprisoned in the realm of the textual is that they are looking for potential narratives in the shelters of written culture. Noticing that nobody has published a grandiose large-scale religion textbook on ecocatastropic-techno-administrative-production systematics, which is endorsed by millions and carried out in the realm of actual praxis by the mighty, our postmodern literary aces brilliantly conclude that "metanarratives are dead."

But metanarratives are not dead. What goes unnoticed by

# theore

of the postmodern is that the style of narratives has

changed since the writing of the Bible,

# Pheno
# gy          of

Effects

and

# capita

First and foremost, the metanarrative of our age is not a written product. The metanarratives of ecocatastrope, the world economy, the technologizing of the lifeworld are not first literary creations that are later materialized. To the contrary, incipient metanarratives involve material practices that have not yet been theorized. Totalization has never been more effective, frightening, universal and penetrating than at the turn of the twenty-first century. The fact that this totalization does not take place initially in the realm of concepts makes it no less significant for anyone other than the theoreticians for whom texts are primary and everything else is secondary.

For the imagologist, the challenge is to think globally without thinking totalistically. Envisioning philosophy as a global project – a large-scale enterprise of universal relevance and consequence – imagology explores two realms that intellectual traditionalists, be they liberal or conservative, avoid at all costs: praxis and the media. In a culture of the simulacrum, textuality becomes a cage. The dynamics of postmodern societies relegate textuality to a secondary position. To join the contemporary debate in a way that fulfills the political and ethical promise of critical engagement, it is necessary to adjust to this new condition – even if this means the rejection of the ancient axiom of philosophy according to which the conceptual, the textual and the written are primary.

ticians

nenolo
Spirit

if information is in the air, where is the foundation?

The rhythm of datawaves marks an oscillation that has become unavoidable. To surf these waves is to realize that erring never ends.

It is important not to confuse information and meaning. Though not precisely opposites, they are inversely proportional: as information increases, meaning decreases. One of the distinctive features of the information age is the proliferation of data whose meaning remains obscure. The more we accumulate the less we have.

We    suffer    and    enjoy    a    delirium    of    information.

Telecommunications technologies constitute the imperative of instantaneous responsibility for which a new, radically diversified, non-disciplined, spontaneous art of perception is necessary. The net result is the emergence of a non-fragmented energy of evaluation and responsibility that creates a sensitivity to context. Contrary to expectation, this radically situational notion of responsibility amounts to humanizing the field of study, techniques of assessment and aims of critical thought.

The    mediatrix    always    disciplines    and    sometimes    punishes.

"Humanitarian" aid in the culture of the simulacrum: While people are starving from Somalia to Bosnia, fans send "care" packages to actors who play impoverished characters on soap operas.

**i**n simcult, the art of sleuthing changes completely. Cyberspace transforms the private eye into an information broker whose window on the world is the

video screen. A Tampa-based outfit named Nationwide Electronic Tracking advertises

# confi dental data 24 hours a day, 7 days a week.

**"**

The information society never sleeps (soundly).

**A** teenager in Atlanta breaks into the telephone company's computer, lifts a file and sends it to an unsuspecting computer phreak in Illinois. The Atlanta hacker stores the file in an obscure location of the Illinois machine where it remains undetected by its owner. A few weeks later, the FBI raids the home of the kid in Illinois and charges him with wire fraud and grand larceny. What is the crime? Who is the criminal? Where is the victim?

**W**ho writes the rules and establishes the laws that govern cyberspace? So far, the regulations in this strange new world are surprisingly few. Entering cyberspace is the closest we can come to returning to the Wild West. Console cowboys roam ranges that seem to extend forever. But as feuds break out, fences are built, cut and rebuilt. Eventually, governments will step in and mess up everything. The wilderness never lasts long – you had better enjoy it before it disappears.

**W**e must address the issue of values that traditional rationalism thinks can be subsumed under abstractions, concepts and institutional rituals. Conventional rationalism maintains its ultra-rigid management methods so strictly that techniques-as-means become ends-in-themselves, thereby destroying the possibility of serious discussion of priorities and values. Ironically, media philosophy, which seems more means- and technology-centered than traditional rationalism, is less technocentric than its critics suppose. Expert culture is so imprisoned in its technologies that even a discussion of fundamental priorities seems out of the question. The logic of the assembly line is, however, forced to question itself when confronted with electronic technology. The usual response is to try to appropriate the electronic. But this effort is doomed to fail because industrial and post-industrial logics are incompatible. We must overthrow assembly-line logic and its philosophy of understanding in order to move toward the interstanding of the electronic age.

**A** revolution in the making: On the net, authors become propertyless.

in 1984, Apple Computer hired Ridley Scott, who directed

# Blade
# Runner,

to develop an advertising campaign for the Macintosh. Must the future

created by personal computers be dystopic, or can another script be written?

**W**hat happens to so-called aesthetic and critical

norms when the hierarchy of print is displaced

by the horizontality of the network ?

At this late hour, we can see that Derrida, with his immense distrust of the conceptual represented through a higher-order conceptuality and a hyper-abstract syntax, is the bridge between the paradigm of conceptually centered philosophy of pure thought and the philosophy of exploding images. As the last and the greatest of the literary philosophers, Derrida is the first syntactician of imagology.

The mediaization of reality threatens the capacity to be shocked. On the surface of the video screen, the extraordinary becomes ordinary, and the horrifying becomes everyday. In the absence of shock, outrage and protest vanish. When nothing is any longer shocking, the avant-garde either disappears or is active everywhere.

In the mediatrix, we can no longer afford the luxury of not asking big questions. The fetishizing of difference is as problematic as the absolutizing of synthesis. What we need are media that provide the means to negotiate the extremes that are tearing us apart.

There is no end to the net. Every destination is a point of departure and every point of departure is a destination. Apparent terminals are actually relays in a circuit that is forever in motion. In simcult, our destiny is to live without destination. We must prevent the absence of destination from creating a sense of purposelessness.

The net is riddled by O zones.

The imagologist issues a call rather than a statement or a

theory.  A call that is a challenge to face up to the radical

changes that are already taking place and to imagine a future

shaped by interstanding.

Globalization involves not only unification and integration but also pluralization and

diversification. The more closely we are related, the more pronounced our differences become.

The task that we face is to find ways to articulate differences without creating oppositions.

## Dear Esa,

Perhaps the "origin" of our
venture goes back even farther than
I previously thought.  You are, of
course, the most American Finnish
philosopher who has ever lived.
Indeed, you might well be the most
American European philosopher who
has ever lived.  But does your
Americanism mean that you are no
longer European? Perhaps.  If, that
is, Baudrillard is right when he
claims that "in Los Angeles, Europe
has disappeared."

LA is America's most postmodern
city.  Indeed, were it not for
Tokyo, LA could claim the title of
the capital of postmodernism - if
everything weren't decapitated in
the postmodern world.

When you came to America to study,

▼

LA was your destination. But
what you learned at UCLA was not
analytic philosophy. That is an
American import from Europe, which
you did not have to cross the
Atlantic to rediscover. Indeed,
America's preoccupation with
analytic philosophy shows the
irrelevance of philosophy in the
contemporary world. Philosophy is
terrified of LA; that is why it
turns back to Europe. What you
discovered in America was LA - the
very LA that philosophy cannot
bear to think. Instead of
deepening your philosophical
interests, LA showed you the
**impossibility** of philosophy.
  The impossibility of philosophy
- until the advent of media
philosophy. To do media
philosophy is to philosophize in
LA and Tokyo while still living in
Helsinki and Williamstown.

●

Gaping

Gaping 1

**A** persistent question repeatedly returns to haunt telecommunications technology: Can everything be processed – digitized, or is there an inescapable remainder, an inevitable excess that always slips away? Though the code dreams of completion, something always seems to exceed its grasp. Does this excess harbor a code that has not yet been discovered or is it a more excessive excess? How might such an excess be thought? Is it too much or too little for codes to capture? If there were such an excess, what would be its place or its non-place?

**A** persistent question repeatedly returns to haunt telecommunications technology: Can everything be processed digitized, or is there an inescapable remainder, an inevitable excess that always slips away? Though the code dreams of completion, something always seems to exceed its grasp. Does this excess harbor a code that has not yet been discovered or is it a more excessive excess? How might such an excess be thought? Is it too much or too little for codes to capture? If there were such an excess, what would be its place or its non-place?

The imagologist is a spacemaker whose task is to create a gap where others can write. For there to be such an opening, everything must remain inconclusive. The absence of answers creates the opening of the media philosopher's quest-ion. The only writing worth reading today is spacey.

Turn on,



tune in,



space out

The digital transmission of audio-visual images requires the transcription of waves into bits that travel at the speed of light. Before anything can be heard or seen, the signal must be decoded or read. Though writing as such is never present, it is, nonetheless, the condition of the possibility of audio-visual images. The non-absent absence of writing insinuates an irreducible distance into the apparent proximity of

speech

and

vision.

**i**magocentrism

is

eccentric

Along the edge of some platforms in the London underground, words of warning that have always fascinated me are painted in big white letters:

# MIND THE GAP.

I first noticed this sign when I was waiting for the train to take me to Freud's reconstructed home on the outskirts of the city. If, as Lacan insists, the unconscious is a gap-like structure, then the admonition to mind the gap might be understood as the most important message of psychoanalysis. But the structure of the gap defines more than the unconscious; consciousness itself is impossible apart from the inarticulate gaps that articulate awareness.

In our explorations of the contemporary mediatrix, we must remain sensitive to the implications of the gap that interrupts discourse. While virtually face-to-face, our conversation is not immediate. Though it is slight, there is an undeniable delay that defers communication. Between the sending and receiving of a message, there is a slippage of approximately 0.25 - 0.5 a second. This delay is a function of the necessity of translating the signal from analog to digital and vice versa. Once the audio and visual signals have been digitized, they travel across fiber optic lines at the speed of light. But translation takes time and this time defers presence. In our effort to emphasize the sophistication of the technology, we must never forget the time of translation. This time is precisely the gap we are called to mind.

The space of the screen is the non-place of the aleatory. The very rigidity of the code makes chance not only possible but unavoidable.

Gaping [5]

Questions opened by the gap:

Did we ever have

what we always lose?

Can we ever hope to possess

what we do not now have?

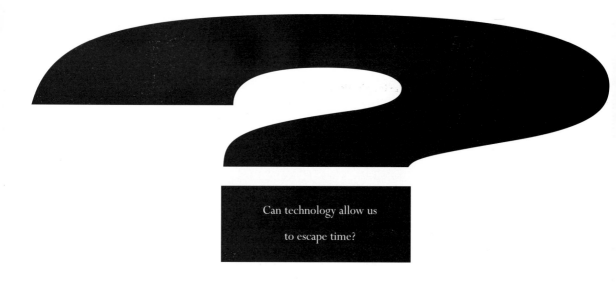

Can technology allow us

to escape time?

Is the dream of presence destined

to remain a dream forever?

The net leaves

Spokespersons for the media unwittingly do precisely what they say they do: they cover events. When we recognize what it means to cover an event, the role of the media must be rethought..

Holes in the net are openings for the imagination.

one a-gap-e

What do **semi**-conductors fail to conduct? What circuits do they leave incomplete? What messages do they leave undelivered? If all conduction is semi-conduction, is true communication ever possible?

# To digitize is to delocalize.

BUT

The imaginary register transforms roots into rhizomes. A rhizomic culture is neither rooted nor unrooted. One can never be sure where rhizomes will break new ground.

# delocalization is not necessarily universalization.

When wires cross, sparks sometimes fly. At the end of the millennium, the world is no closer to peace than it was at the beginning of the twentieth century.

**W**hen you lose the sense of death, it is no longer necessary or possible to philosophize in traditional ways. Philosophy ends when death dies. The death of death is not its disappearance but its forgetting. In simcult, death has receded in oblivion through the play of images, which, paradoxically, stages death's incessant arrival. In the absence of death, classical philosophy becomes impossible and thus it is necessary to invent new ways of philosophizing.

T h e

task

image [imidʒ] I s 1 [veisto]kuva; (erik) jumalankuva, pyhimyksenkuva; ~ with feet of clay savijaloilla seisova jättiläinen 2 (optinen) kuva; peili-, heijastus|kuva 3 näköisyys, kuva; created (made) in God's ~ luotu Jumalan kuvaksi; he is the very ~ of his father hän on ilmetty isänsä 4 mieli-, muisti|kuva 5 perikuva (she is the ~ of devotion) 6 kielikuva, metafora (speak in ~s) 7 kuvitelma 8 imago; yrityskuva II tr 1 kuvata 2 kuvastaa 3 ~ [to o.s.] kuvitella 4 kuvailla, kuvata eloisasti 5 symboloida.

that remains after the death of God is to learn to believe in nothing. As Buddhists have long realized, belief in nothing is far from nihilistic.

There is an urgent need for an electronic environmentalism. Our responsibility to our children and future generations must include not only the preservation of the so-called natural environment but also the responsible enrichment of the electronic environment. The living space that is becoming our world is as much electronic as natural. The matrix in all of its embodiments must be cultivated.

Intervention in the imaginary register presupposes a certain "exteriority" to networks "within" which we are nonetheless inscribed. Responsible action within the structures that constitute our worlds must always be undertaken from an "outside" that is "inside." The pulse of this interior exterior or exterior interior cannot be digitized but registers as *care* that appears to be groundless. Care "is" the gap in the mediatrix that makes its constitution and reconstitution possible.

1 **wire** [waiə*] *s* 1 [metalli-, teräs-, rauta]lanka; vanunki 2 (sähkö-, puhelin- ym) johto; lanka; johdin 3 vaijeri; kaapeli 4 (ark) puhelin; *on the* ~ langalla, langan päässä 5 (erik Am) a) sähke; b) lennätin; *by* ~ sähkeitse 6 piikkilanka-aita; teräs-, rauta|lankaverkko 7 [ansa]lanka 8 (mus) metalli-, teräs|kieli 9 (Am hevosurh) maaliviiva 10 (pap) viira 11 (sl) taskuvaras ▶ **down to the** ~ (erik Am ark) a) viime hetkeen (viimeiseen) saakka; lähellä loppua; b) rahat melkein lopussa; **get one's** ~**s crossed** (ark) käsittää väärin; **pull** ~**s** (kuv) pitää lankoja käsissään; juonitella, vehkeillä; **under the** ~ a) (hevosurh) maaliviivalla; b) (kuv) viime hetkellä (tingassa), juuri ajoissa; *get in under the* ~ ehtiä viime hetkellä.
2 **wire** [waiə*] *tr* ja *itr* 1 kiinnittää (tukea) metallilangalla; langoittaa 2 aidata, erottaa [piikki]langalla 3 ~ *[up]* (sähk, rak) vetää (asentaa) jnnk sähkö[johdot], johdottaa *(a house);* liittää (johto) 4 (mets) pyytää langoilla 5 sähköttää [jklle] *(mother was* ~*d for),* lähettää jklle sähke; lähettää sähkeitse *(money)* 6 ~ *[up]* (TV) vetää kaapeli[t] jhk; liittää [kaapeli]verkkoon 7 pujottaa (helmiä) lankaan 8 (kroketti) *be* ~*d* joutua porttilangan (t. kepin) taakse 9 a) asentaa sala-kuuntelulaitteita jhk; b) asentaa murto-hälytin jhk 10 ~ *in* (ark) käydä jhk käsiksi; hyökätä jnk kimppuun.

# Trans atlant ic Cab les:

**December 10, 1992**

# the fir st of t he ex chang

**Mark:**

# e

Our "book" will, in a certain sense, be a non-book. It should not be limited by the linear logic of the past, which urges the reader to proceed from the first page to the second, and then continue in the order marked by page numbering, from left to right, down and up, following page-turning conventions all the way to the end. Like a hypertext, the reader should be free to chart alternative courses through the wordmass we fabricate. The work must also be riddled with gaps, spaces and openings that invite the reader to write. White space becomes the site of transaction in which the event of understanding occurs. In different terms, the book of media philosophy must become a notebook or a workbook. To the reader, who is a writer, we say: "Come, join us in a process of writing-reading/reading-writing in which all production is reproductive coproduction."

**A**s I look toward Europe and you look toward the States, where do we meet? What do we create?

# what then?

*Surely not a synthesis.*

*Nor an analysis.*

Something other.    Something else.    Something that is still searching for a name. · · ▶

▶ Will we find that name before finishing this text? Even after finishing this unfinnishable text?

**MEDIATEXT
A collection of
f a b r i c s
designed    by
Marjaana Virta
for  Marimekko**

# marimekko®

Head Office, Finland    Germany    Contact in the USA

Marimekko Oy    Marimekko GmbH    Donna Gorman Inc.
Puusepänkatu 4    Rheinstrasse 19    1 Marshall Street
00810 Helsinki    60325 Frankfurt/Main    South Norwalk, CT 06854
Tel. +358 0 75871    Tel. (069) 749084    Tel. (203) 831-9487
Fax +358 0 7553051    Fax (069) 742643    Fax (203) 831-9489